DIRT RIDER's
MOTOCROSS RIDING TIPS

BY THE EDITORS OF DIRT RIDER® MAGAZINE

MBI Publishing Company

First published in 2002 by MBI Publishing Company, Galtier Plaza, Suite 200, 380 Jackson Street, St. Paul, MN 55101-3885 USA

MBI Publishing Company books are also available at discounts in bulk quantity for industrial or sales-pro-motional use. For details write to Special Sales Manager at Motorbooks International Wholesalers & Distributors, Galtier Plaza, Suite 200, 380 Jackson Street, St. Paul, MN 55101-3885 USA.

On the front cover: Travis Pastrana on the number 199 factory Suzuki RM250 at the 2002 San Diego Supercross. Travis finished second behind Yamaha-mounted David Vuillemin. Ken Faught

On the back cover: Ricky Carmichael on the 2002 factory Honda CR250. Ken Faught

Library of Congress Cataloging-in-Publication Data Available
ISBN 0-7603-1315-6

Edited by Lee Klancher

Printed in the United States of America

Contents

Foreword By Lee Klancher 5

Chapter ONE

Starts 6
Jeremy McGrath's holeshot tips 7
Steve Hatch on holeshots 8
Line choices 10
How to avoid getting buried in the pack 11
Downhill starts 12
RC and concrete starts 13

Chapter TWO

Turns 14
Steve Lamson on maintaining momentum in turns 15
Larry Ward on railing sand berms .16
McGrath on technical cornering technique 17
Dick Burleson: Standing-to-seated transitions for turns 18
Randy Hawkins: Aggressive woods cornering tactics 19
Kevin Hines: Avoid those trees in turns 20
McGrath on midair turning 21
McGrath on accelerating out of turns 22
Undercut banked turns with Scott Summers 23
How to tackle nasty corners with Jeff Fredette 24
Scott Summers on downhill ruts leading into a turn 25
Cornering: Open your eyes! 26
Steve Hatch on turns in tight woods 27
Cutting Corners by Damon Huffman 28
Cooper on ultra-high-speed turns .30
Emig on negotiating rutted turns .31
Brake slide turns with Mike Lafferty 32
Emergency line changes wth Mike LaRocco 33
Save energy with Steve Hatch 34
Taking on flat, slick corners with Jeremy McGrath 35
Sticking flat corners with jumps by Scott Hoffman 36
Scott Summers root avoidance 101 .37

Chapter THREE

Jumps 38
Steve Lamson: How to attack uphill jumps 39
Ryan Hughes: Conquering tiered uphill doubles 40
McGrath on taming uneven whoops 41
Lamson on not doing doubles 42
When you don't clear that double .43
How Steve Lamson handles jumps with kicker lips 44
Jeff Emig on tackling rutted jumps 45
Ty Davis tells when it's best to roll, not jump 46
Jeff Emig on front-wheel landings .47
Downhill doubles with John Dowd .48
Flying low by Jeremy McGrath 49
Kevin Windham on making the inside line 50

Michael Craig on small seat-bounce jumps 51
Larry Ward on skipping across obstacles 52
Soaking up small jumps with Tallon Vohland 53
Anatomy of the perfect jump with Nathan Ramsey 55
Airing out off-road with Ty Davis 56
Drop-Offs with Kevin Windham 57

Chapter FOUR   **Hot Tips** **58**
Jeremy McGrath: Braking tricks 59
ISDE Training camp 60
Powder surfing 62
Guy Cooper riding tip handbook 63
Larry Roeseler and Ty Davis on team tactics and desert racing 69
Paul Edmondson on how to wheelie 70
Cold weather riding tips 71
Dick Burleson on Braking 74
Hot weather riding tips 75
The champs guide to play riding 76
Guy Cooper on line choice 79
Back to basics by Gary Semics 80
Suspension S.O.S. 82
Prepare for muddy days 87
Sand washes with Destry Abbott 88
How to handle whoops 89
Doing the dab 90
Deep rutted tracks 91
Maintain drive with standing wheelies 92
Night Advice 93
Speed Secrets 95

Chapter FIVE   **Trails** **104**
Kevin Hines: Bounding through boulder fields 105
Guy Cooper: How to avoid hang-ups on logs 106
Kevin Hines on single-track off-camber trails 107
Scott Summers' riding tip handbook 108
Dick Burleson on crossing big, angled logs 111
Kevin Hines with slalom speed secrets for woods racers 112
Dick Burleson on small-log crossings 113
Randy Hawkins on uphill switchbacks 114
Lafferty takes on drop-offs 115
Mastering mud ditches 116
Johnny Campbell attacks high-speed G-outs 117
Thinking wet 118
Riding high-speed fire roads with Johnny Campbell 119

Chapter SIX   **Hills** **120**
Ty Davis: Squat to scale slick, steep hills .121
Kevin Hines: Uphill rock jump 122
Dick Burleson: Simple stairstep techniques 123
Hawkins on clutch-control climbs 124
Downhills with Destry Abbott 125
Turning on a hill you can't climb with Ty Davis 126

Index **127**

Foreword

Ten years ago, I finally graduated from college and had enough money and time to get back into off-road racing, one of the great loves of my life. I bought a 1989 KX250 from a vet racer and promptly took it up to my family's cabin for an early March ride.

The ground was hard and frozen with patches of snow and ice on the ground. I was dressed in the traditional small town boy race gear—blue jeans, work boots, a flannel shirt, leather work gloves, and a new, used lid (a Moto 4 with green and blue graphics). I had been riding street bikes for the past seven years, which meant my experience with explosive, peaky, light motorcycles consisted of murky memories from my high school years.

Well, the results were predictable. The bike hit hard, fast, and low. Traction was nil. I sat back on the bike, like you do on a street bike. I could have been the poster boy for Geek Riding. Needless to say, I spent a lot of time on the ground. By the end of the day, the pocket was torn off my jeans, my helmet was scuffed, I had a giant raspberry on my forearm, and my ego was bruised.

A few months later, I found myself on the starting line at the local motocross track in Cambridge, Minnesota. The track is a sandpit with turns and a few weak attempts at jumps, and then more deep sand. I spent the better part of that race picking up the bike, and there wasn't many people behind me when I was done.

At this point, I knew I needed some help. I found that the best thing to do was ride. The more I did, the better I performed. Another thing that really helped me out was a piece in Dirt Rider magazine about body positioning. From that one article, I found out that my biggest problem was where I was placing my body on the bike. By moving forward and raising my elbows, I had more control of the motorcycle.

That one example stands out, but through experience, advice, and reading about riding, I slowly improved. Today I can proudly say I'm the slowest guy in a reasonably quick group of riders. It feels great to be on the bike, and I know I can get through pretty much any kind of terrain out there. My riding isn't perfect, but I can get through the race and maybe even pass a guy now and again.

My point is that this collection of articles will make you a better rider if you pay attention and try out the techniques. The pros know what to do to go fast and win. The more thoughtful fast guys—Scott Summers and Randy Hawkins come to mind—have a lot of good advice for everyone from the dual-sport weekend rider to the A rider who wants to make the cut at a Pro National.

I hope you enjoy the articles that have been selected, and that you learn a few techniques to help you out on the trail. Ride hard, have fun, and throw lots of roost.

—Lee Klancher
St. Paul, Minnesota

Starts

CHAPTER ONE

Jeremy McGrath's holeshot tips 7
Steve Hatch on holeshots 8
Line choices 10
How to avoid getting buried in the pack 11
Downhill starts 12
RC and concrete starts 13

JEREMY McGRATH'S HOLESHOT TIPS

Getting to the first turn ahead of the pack is by far the single most important move you can perform on the race track. The biggest advantage is that you have a clear, dust- and roost-free track, which allows *you* to set the pace. Plus, you don't have to worry about passing (except for lappers) when you get a holeshot. You can simply concentrate on going faster, riding smoothly and riding your own race.

To explain the fine art of this masterful technique, we couldn't think of anyone better than Honda's Jeremy McGrath. During his rookie year, McGrath's incredible holeshot ability is said to have been the single most important ingredient to winning his first supercross championship. Here's McGrath to explain how it's done.

1 "The start begins with gate selection," McGrath points out. "Make sure that you have a straight shot to the first turn and that there are no rocks or mud in your line. Then, when staging, I try to visualize a perfect start in my head. I slide as forward as possible on the seat, lean over the handlebar with my elbows up, stick the bike in second gear, pull in the front brake with one finger, let the clutch out until the bike starts to grab, turn the throttle approximately half open and then watch the gate. Right before the gate is ready to drop, I concentrate on the [mechanism] pin beneath the gate. This is the first sign that the gate is ready to drop."

2 "As the gate drops, let out the clutch slowly to avoid too much wheelspin," McGrath instructs. "You don't want to drop the clutch or you'll never get traction. I'm at least five feet out of the gate before my clutch lever is fully released and the throttle is pinned."

3 "Because of the good traction, the bike will always want to wheelie—unless you're in sand or mud," McGrath cautions. "To minimize this problem, keep your weight over the handlebar as long as you can." Notice that McGrath actually arches his back to get more of his weight on the front end of his bike. Also notice that, with the exception of Jimmy Button (20), who's also got a good start, all the other riders have already started to sit upright.

4 "Before you begin to sit up, you want to make sure that you're ahead of the rest of the guys," McGrath continues. "Usually, I start upshifting and sliding back on the seat once my elbows are clearly ahead of everyone else's handlebars. This way, I don't get pinched off down the start straight or in the first turn. I also aim toward the inside line so I don't get stuffed and because most crashes happen in the middle or outside of the first turn."

STEVE HATCH ON HOLESHOTS

Most off-road races begin with a dead-engine start. In an enduro, a muffed holeshot on a line with only three other riders is only a temporary inconvenience. But at a desert race or Grand National Cross Country event, a slow start means a lot of serious work at best and a personal safety hazard at worst. The best plan is to avoid the problem with a holeshot. Just one hitch, only one guy can holeshot at a time. At the majority of GNCC races this year, Steve Hatch has been the guy up front at each start. Inquiring minds wanted to know: How does he do it against the best, most experienced riders in the country?

1 At the Moose Run in Illinois, Hatch only had a Cycra bike stand, but for actual races he uses a Cycra starting step like this one. He gives it much of the credit for getting to the first turn first. The aluminum teeth dig into the ground, giving the rider a solid foundation to stand on and push off of. A regular motorcycle stand is too tall and doesn't grip the ground well enough.

2 Hatch starts his RM250's engine and lets it warm to operating temperature. Then if the race venue allows it, he rides the bike and gets the engine under a load to make sure it runs clean and strong. Don't just sit with the engine running until start time. The liquid-cooled engine can't cool efficiently while sitting still, and a hot engine doesn't make the best power for the start. It needs to be at operating temperature, but after the safety point, cooler is better than hotter.

3 A minute or two before the race is about to begin, the starter signals the riders to shut down the engines. Before shutting down, Hatch holds the rear brake on tight, then loads the engine against the brake by easing out the clutch till it drags hard and pulls the engine rpm down. After doing that a couple of times to clean out the engine, Hatch hits the kill button and holds the throttle wide open as the engine winds down. He keeps the bike in the gear he'll start in and holds the clutch lever in all the way while killing the engine. He *never* releases the clutch lever until the engine is restarted for the race. These steps minimize the drag of the clutch plates while the engine is kicked through and charges the cylinders and cases for a quick start.

PHOTOS: KAREL KRAMER

4 As start time nears, Hatch readies himself for a full kick and a healthy push-off from the Cycra stand. He folds out the starter but doesn't touch it with his foot. He doesn't crank it through or even check to make sure it's on the compression stroke. He rests his boot against the seat to keep his foot from putting any premature pressure on the lever. The clutch lever is still in, and in the last few seconds he raises his head and concentrates on the starter. Hatch is always in the first row, so he can't watch the starter during other starts. But if you have the opportunity, watch other starts to see if the starter somehow signals that he is about to move, so you can better anticipate your start.

6 Hatch hasn't fully weighted the seat yet. The kickstarter hasn't even folded up, but he's in attack position, the throttle's wide open and the rear wheel's spinning. Note that his push-off already puts the bike slightly ahead of the stand. At this point, the key is to assume an exaggerated attack position and keep the front end down in the excellent traction the line offers.

5 When Hatch sees the flag hint at movement, he stomps down on the kickstarter, opens the throttle and pushes off hard with his left leg. He claims that even if the engine didn't start, he would still be five feet down course just from the push-off! Note that he has his weight well forward to aid in pushing off and keeping the bike from wheelying when the engine fires and the clutch is released. He also has his head up and is looking at where he wants to go.

7 As Hatch leaves the line, he moves his weight back to increase traction. Notice that his throttle hand hasn't changed. He has the throttle open and controls the power and traction with the clutch and his body position.

8 Farther out from the starting line, Hatch still searches for optimum drive. The clutch is almost all the way out, and he controls a very low-power wheelie with his body position. He keeps the bike straight, doesn't allow radical wheelies or wheelspin, and if other bikes were here, he would be well on his way to another holeshot!

PHOTOS: KAREL KRAMER

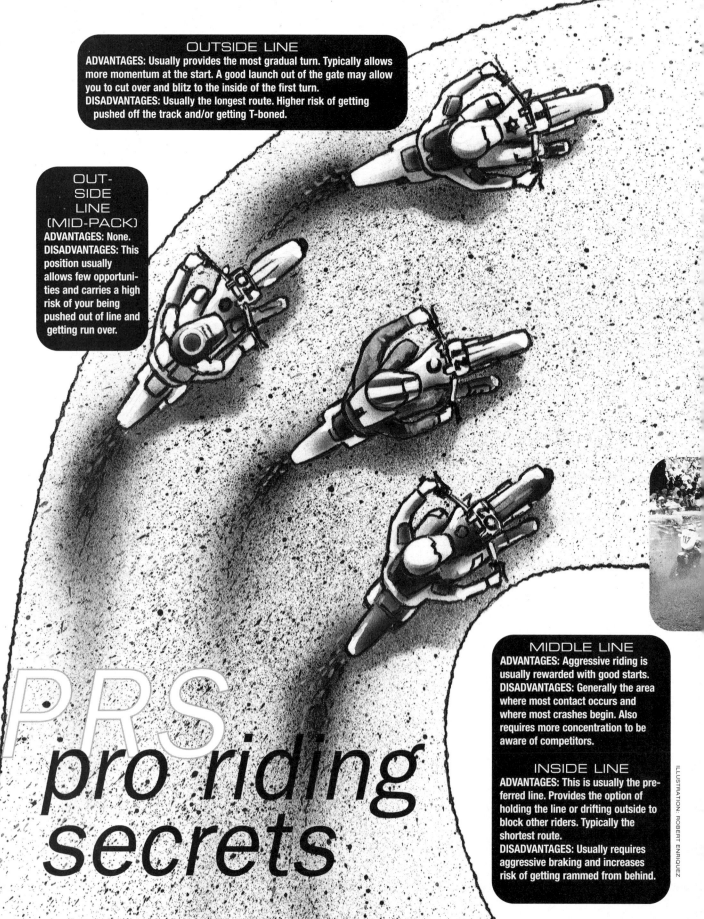

OUTSIDE LINE
ADVANTAGES: Usually provides the most gradual turn. Typically allows more momentum at the start. A good launch out of the gate may allow you to cut over and blitz to the inside of the first turn.
DISADVANTAGES: Usually the longest route. Higher risk of getting pushed off the track and/or getting T-boned.

OUT-SIDE LINE (MID-PACK)
ADVANTAGES: None.
DISADVANTAGES: This position usually allows few opportunities and carries a high risk of your being pushed out of line and getting run over.

MIDDLE LINE
ADVANTAGES: Aggressive riding is usually rewarded with good starts.
DISADVANTAGES: Generally the area where most contact occurs and where most crashes begin. Also requires more concentration to be aware of competitors.

INSIDE LINE
ADVANTAGES: This is usually the preferred line. Provides the option of holding the line or drifting outside to block other riders. Typically the shortest route.
DISADVANTAGES: Usually requires aggressive braking and increases risk of getting rammed from behind.

PRS
pro riding secrets

HOW TO AVOID GETTING BURIED IN THE PACK

Surviving a first turn is one of the toughest things a racer can accomplish on a routine basis. Most first turns are danger zones full of psychotic throttle junkies who turn their motorcycles into 50-horsepower projectiles. Though luck is a factor, there are a lot of tricks that can improve your chances of survival. Of course they vary depending on the type of turn and subsequent obstacles, but they do provide a good foundation.

Generally, the inside line is preferred. The rider in this position sets the tempo and dictates how other riders respond. It's usually best to hug the inside of the turn to set up for the next obstacle, and the rider on the inside line has the most options. If he has a good start and realizes someone has cut up the middle or is sweeping to the outside, he can drift wide to block. This can be rather dangerous, but it can also be very effective. The rider on the inside, though, must watch out. He runs the greatest risk of getting his front wheel clipped and being run over by half the pack.

Riders in the middle tend to be the most aggressive. This spot requires a lot of confidence and generously rewards risk takers. As riders funnel into the first turn, those in the middle are forced to make a rather big decision: stay on the throttle and gamble on carrying a lot of speed through the turn, or get pinched off and be forced to settle for a mid-pack start. This position is typically where most crashes occur, but it's not the most dangerous one.

This honor is reserved for the outside line because of its high speeds. Some riders like to rail the outside of first turns because it offers the

There are no excuses for dead last starts. The first lap of any race always sets the tone and it's hard to get motivated when you're in 40th place.

most gradual turn, but this area fills up fast and riders are often pushed out of the turn and off the track.

Only you can assess the risk and the possible rewards of a particular line. But if you want to win races, the start is a great place to gain the upper hand.

This is a classic example of a rider getting pushed out of his line. Number 94 has no choice but to brush off speed by drifting wide.

Fear, not a lack of talent, may be the biggest limiting factor in overcoming poor starts. If you want to get the holeshot, focus on success, not failure.

pro riding secrets

DOWNHILL STARTS

Seventy-five percent of the time, races are won and lost at the starting gate. Catlike reflexes combined with precise body positioning and clutch and throttle control dictate the jump out of the gate. If the rear tire spins too much or if there is not enough power to the ground, a rider can lose inches at the start that transmit to feet and yards by the first turn. Problem is, just when you think you have the process licked, different variables get thrown into the mix. Changing circumstances require changing processes. Here we investigate the finer points of the downhill start.

This start has a four-foot drop right out of the gate. Knowing this, a rider must change his starting procedure slightly before the gate drops, keeping his weight as far forward as possible and controlling the clutch. If a rider comes out of the gate as if this were a normal start, chances are the front would wheelie too high when the rear wheel hits the drop. In this case, a rider would have to chop the throttle or use excessive amounts of clutch to correct the problem. Mike LaRocco (5) is starting correctly: His front wheel is on the ground.

In this photo, the bikes are fully over the crest of the start and are powering down the slight grade. To keep the front wheel down, most riders had to keep their body weight forward longer than normal and had to slip the clutch more than usual. LaRocco had better clutch control coming out of the start and this kept the wheel lower. As soon as he got the bike over the crest, he could get on the gas harder than the riders who were still fighting to keep the wheel low.

By the time the riders hit the bottom of the grade they will be under full power. Riders who have made the best use of throttle and clutch control will get the best drive into the tight first turn. Notice how staggered the riders are at this point. This is the difference a good jump out of the gate makes.

12

pro riding secrets

RC AND CONCRETE STARTS

It's a well-known fact that starts are one of the most important elements to winning races. Getting a poor launch out of the blocks almost guarantees a mid-pack or even worse position at the beginning of a race. The combination of concentration, quick reflexes and proper technique is key to getting a jump on the field. Ricky Carmichael's dominance in the 125 class is partly because of his catlike reflexes and his precise technique when it comes to gating on concrete backward-falling starts. Follow RC as he demonstrates a textbook start from a concrete launch pad.

The first series of photos is what really matters: the initial launch out of the gate. As you can see from the rear tire, Carmichael didn't do a huge burnout prior to the start. Some riders go hog-wild and lay down a large amount of rubber on the ground. RC heats up the tire just enough to put a little rubber on the ground and scuff any dirt off the tire.

In the first photo, the gate has just hit the ground; Carmichael is centered on the seat in a semiupright position to keep as much weight on the rear wheel as possible. Most 125 riders use first gear to start, while some really light racers can get away with second; 250 pilots almost always use second gear.

The second photo was taken during the critical stages of a concrete start. Too much throttle and clutch can cause the tire to spin, while too little throttle and clutch feed can result in the bike bogging. This is where practice and knowing the power delivery of a bike are important. Practice smoothly slipping the clutch to create the least amount of wheelspin when the gate drops.

In the final shot of this series, RC is still feeding power to the ground via the throttle and clutch while staying centered on the bike to keep it tracking straight. Also notice he's already starting to lift his left foot to the peg for a quick shift to the next gear.

Check out Carmichael: Before he even hits the dirt, his left foot is on the peg and ready to shift. As soon as his rear wheel hits the dirt, RC will grab another gear. Some riders like Jeremy McGrath keep their feet forward at the start and use the heel of the boot to grab the next gear. We don't suggest trying this move without a lot of practice.

In the second photo, Carmichael already has a six- to eight-inch jump on the field. Notice he uses a little body English to counterweight the fact he has lifted his left foot to the peg faster than the right. Keeping the bike straight before it hits the dirt will translate to maximum drive into the first turn. Also notice RC has already transferred his weight back on the seat to get the best bite in the dirt.

In the final photo, you can see the larger roost coming from his rear tire as he motors away with the holeshot.

[FACT] KTM's Kevin Hines won the 1989 Tecate 250K Enduro in Mexico.

PHOTOS: DONNIE BALES

Turns

CHAPTER TWO

Steve Lamson on maintaining momentum in turns 15
Larry Ward on railing sand berms 16
McGrath on technical cornering technique 17
Dick Burleson: Standing-to-seated transitions for turns 18
Randy Hawkins: Aggressive woods cornering tactics 19
Kevin Hines: Avoid those trees in turns. 20
McGrath on midair turning 21
McGrath on accelerating out of turns 22
Undercut banked turns with Scott Summers 23
How to tackle nasty corners with Jeff Fredette 24
Scott Summers on downhill ruts leading into a turn 25
Cornering: Open your eyes! 26
Steve Hatch on turns in tight woods 27
Cutting Corners by Damon Huffman 28
Cooper on ultra-high-speed turns 30
Emig on negotiating rutted turns 31
Brake slide turns with Mike Lafferty 32
Emergency line changes wth Mike LaRocco 33
Save energy with Steve Hatch. 34
Taking on flat, slick corners with Jeremy McGrath 35
Sticking flat corners with jumps by Scott Hoffman 36
Scott Summers root avoidance 101 37

STEVE LAMSON ON MAINTAINING MOMENTUM IN TURNS

Cornering speed is usually the single, most important ingredient to becoming a better overall rider. It's the one piece of the speed puzzle that ties everything together. For example: Faster cornering speed may allow you to get enough drive to jump a double that you wouldn't normally be able to make successfully. Greater cornering speed also gives you more opportunities to pass, both by braking later and accelerating earlier.

The importance of cornering speed is even more critical on smaller, less-powerful bikes and when navigating uphills. This became obvious during the '95 Motocross des Nations in Slovakia, as Honda's Steve Lamson tried to finesse his way around the hill-and-valley circuit. Here he is to explain his technique of carrying more momentum.

1 "This turn is extremely wide, which allows a variety of line choices," Lamson begins. "I approach the turn much like a roadracer, intending to make a very gradual turn. The key is to make the turn as straight as possible, which will help keep cornering speed up. The sharper the turn, the more momentum you'll have to sacrifice."

"I begin by drifting way outside with the intention of hitting the rut at the bottom. I do all my braking earlier than normal so I can stay off the brakes once I begin to lean the bike over. This is important because part of the turn is off-camber and any braking in the turn could cause you to slide out. Once the braking is over, I sit down, slide forward on the seat, stick out my inside leg and weight the outside peg."

"The downside of this approach is that it sets you up to be stuffed. Always watch out for guys trying to dive down on the inside. They'll be able to reach the turn before you, but they'll have a more difficult time braking and will have to square off the turn, destroying all their momentum."

2 "In this photo I'm beginning to turn, but my body position hasn't changed much," Lamson says. "As I set up for the turn, notice that I don't lean the bike over too much. That's because you have to steer with the throttle to help get the bike pointed in the right direction. At this stage, clutch and throttle control are important because you want to avoid wheelspin. Wheelspin will only increase the chances of sliding out."

3 "At the bottom of the turn, there's a rut that helps provide a lot of resistance," Lamson points out. "On approach, I always try to match up the angle of both my wheels with the angle of the rut. This step is also really important because it will determine whether you've done an effective job of braking. If you go into the turn too fast and have to hit the brakes, the bike will stand up in the turn and you could high-side. You could also blow right through the rut or several other things that wouldn't do you much good."

4 "Once both wheels are firmly seated in the rut, you're safe to get on the gas hard," Lamson continues. "Don't get on the gas too fast, otherwise you risk wheelying out of the turn, which may cause you to momentarily lose control. At this point, you should keep your head up and begin looking towards the next obstacle."

PHOTOS: KEN FAUGHT

pro riding secrets MOTO

LARRY WARD ON RAILING SAND BERMS

There is a distinct talent to riding in sand. Those who have a good grasp of the concept excel at this unique skill; those who don't simply flounder hopelessly.

Interestingly enough, in the hard-pack-dominated world of supercross, there was such a sand turn immediately before a 70-foot triple jump in Paris. In order to get enough speed to safely clear the jump, riders had to rail the turn with surgical precision. Here's Larry Ward to explain.

1 "Typically, you want to enter a sand berm just like you would a rutted turn," Ward begins. "You want to line your wheels up with the entrance of the turn so you can make a smooth arc. Do all of your braking before the turn so that you enter the berm at a safe turning speed. If you do need additional stopping power, only use the rear brake. If you grab onto the front brake and have started to lean over, the front end will either plow or the bike will stand straight up."

2 "At this point, I'm just finishing my braking and am starting to lean over," Ward continues. "I slide my weight forward, keep my elbows up and get ready to accelerate. Because the sand robs so much power, you can be more aggressive with throttle application. You don't want too much, however: You could dig in and lose momentum, or it could cause the front wheel to push."

3 "As you can see by my roost, I get on the throttle shortly before the apex of the turn," Ward points out. "The most important aspect is to make your turn gradual and conform with your original arc, keep your inside leg out and keep your eyes focused ahead."

4 "Upon exiting the turn, it's safe to open the throttle as much as you like," Ward allows. "Only after you're pointed completely straight should you put your foot back on the footpeg."

McGRATH ON TECHNICAL CORNERING TECHNIQUE

Sometimes you must seek an alternative line in order to make a pass. Such was the case during the Paris supercross when Honda's Jeremy McGrath had to use an extreme inside line to get around this slower rider.

The line McGrath chose was difficult for many reasons, most of which had to do with the slick, rut- and berm-free surface that provided little traction. The line also required a tighter turn than did the more gradual outside line, which made it more tricky. Here's McGrath to explain:

1 "The key to making this work is patience," McGrath begins. "Even though you have the shortest route, the outside in this case has a good banking that allows for more aggressive riding and higher speeds. One of the most common mistakes riders make is accelerating too hard, which causes the rear wheel to slide out."

2 "Patience is also required while braking," McGrath continues. "If you get too aggressive, you'll blow your rhythm. The whole trick is being smooth. Before you reach the apex, make sure your weight is over the front of the bike and weight the outside footpeg so the wheels will hook up better. At this point, try to avoid additional braking with the front brake, because it could cause the front end to wash out."

3 "Now you have to make a decision," McGrath determines. "The fastest line would be to maintain the inside, but if that doesn't look like it's going to work, you may consider taking the other rider's line. In most cases you'll make some contact and even risk crashing, but it's an option if you find there's no other way to pass."

4 "As you can see, it appears that I have actually passed him, when, in fact, the pass isn't totally complete," McGrath insists. "He's got more momentum on the outside, which means I have to make sure I don't make any mistakes during my exit. This will set me up to make the actual pass on the next obstacle."

5 "My drive in this instance was good enough to match his speed going into the next obstacle, which is a whoop section," McGrath says. "At this point we are dead even. Now it's up to me to make sure I can beat him to the next turn."

17

DICK BURLESON: STANDING-TO-SEATED TRANSITIONS FOR TURNS

When riding fast through relatively open sections of woods trails, you'll most likely be standing because it allows you to see farther ahead, make corrections quicker and absorb unseen bumps better.

At the end of every straightaway (however short it may be) lies a turn, and if it's a tight one, it's usually better to be sit-ting down to go through it quickly. We figured Dick Burleson could shed some light on the subtleties of transitioning from a standing to a seated position based on the experience derived from winning eight consecutive AMA National Enduro Championships. Your height doesn't seem to matter, though taller riders will expend a bit more energy.

1 "As I approach [the corner], I'm fully standing," Burleson says. "I accelerate pretty late into the turn, and I'm looking up ahead to see where this thing goes. It's a 90-degree right-hander with a cou-ple of trees on the outside and a tree on the inside, so you have to be precise with your line. Coming down into the corner, I transfer my weight back as I start to brake, keeping my legs pretty straight so I can let the bike's suspension work—it's always bumpy where peo-ple are braking. So your weight is way back, but your butt's up pret-ty high to let the rear of the bike work, and you're pushing the front end down so you can get more traction in the front for braking."

2 "Once I've got my speed pretty much down to where I'm gonna make the turn, I stop holding myself back against the footpegs and the seat, let myself come forward and drop down into the seat. That's right before the turn. Don't come down while you're still brak-ing; you brake hard while standing because that's how you get the best braking."

3 "At the turn itself, I'm in the seat and pretty far forward against the gas tank."

4 "I have to look, twisting my upper body just a little bit, to see where the trail goes."

RANDY HAWKINS
AGGRESSIVE WOODS CORNERING TACTICS

Races are defined as speed contests—he who maintains the highest speed wins the contest. Enduro courses throw all sorts of things at you to slow you down, from tightly spaced trees to tricky hills and treacherous turns.

Here, Suzuki's Randy Hawkins shares his secrets for aggressive cornering in a dry, off-camber corner. As a five-time AMA National Enduro Champion, he's developed an explosive, yet controlled, style that gets him through turns with a minimum of lost speed.

1 "I've just reached the [apex] of this turn," Hawkins says. "My body is forward, and I'm starting to use the clutch. I start to weight the outside [peg], and I use my left leg for balance."

2 "My body is really forward, and my left [foot] serves as a pivot point. I use the clutch to snap or spin the bike around the corner but avoid spinning out of control."

3 "My body is still forward to keep the front of the bike down while I leave the corner. I drag my left [foot] to help keep my body and the bike in control because I'm a little off-balance. Dragging your [foot] in a slow corner works well, but in a fast corner it's not a good idea," he cautions.

4 "I accelerate hard out of the corner with my weight forward, both for control and to keep the [front end] on the ground. I look ahead to prepare for my next obstacle."

Of course, sometimes even the best make mistakes. "I screwed up here," Hawkins admits. "My weight is back, the bike is wheelying, and I have little control for the next corner—*but I look good!* This is how most pro off-road racers ride." Sure, Randy.

pro riding secrets
ENDURO

KEVIN HINES
AVOID THOSE TREES IN TURNS

Why is it that woods trails are typically a series of short straightaways interrupted by trees? Because you're riding in the woods! Trees are what it's all about, and the more skilled you become at dodging them, the faster you'll be able to go.

Former AMA National Enduro Champion Kevin Hines hones his tree-dodging skills almost daily near his Massachusetts home. We asked what he'd suggest to improve our ability and pass his tips on to you. "Keeping the bike upright and focusing ahead is the most important thing about this corner," he summarizes.

"The most important thing is setting up for this corner, [and that begins] at the last corner, which, I'd say, is 40 or 50 feet back. You want to look ahead as soon as you hit the apex of the [last] corner; you want to focus on the next apex. There's a tree on the inside of the [next] corner, so that presents some problems: You can't lean the bike over and just rail the berm.

"Set up a little bit wider than you otherwise [would] and weight the outside foot heavily while keeping the bike upright. You don't want to lean it over too far. I hit my [rear] brake hard to almost slide the rear end out to set up for this.

"I don't recommend this for all corners, but for this situation I think it's real important to slide the rear end a little and then point your front end back out of the corner. You want to be on the gas as early as you can, of course, because it's a race from corner to corner."

1 Hines has already determined what he needs to do at the approaching corner because he saw it while exiting the previous one. Look ahead at all times.

2 He's on the brakes entering the corner, barely locking up the rear to slide the back of the bike a bit to help keep it more vertical and avoid the trees on the inside of the turn. "I'm not leaned over too far because I'd hit the handlebar," he notes.

3 "I'm sitting or raised off the seat just a tiny bit [through the corner]—not fully standing because that would be too awkward. You have to keep your center of gravity down in this situation." Instead of leaning the bike, he leans his body into the corner while still avoiding the trees on the inside.

4 Hines returns to the standing position as he exits the corner and is under full acceleration. With no trees to the inside to worry about, he leans the bike a little more and, of course, is looking down the trail to the next obstacle.

20

McGRATH ON MIDAIR TURNING

When a jump precedes a turn, it transforms two ordinarily simple obstacles into a much more difficult challenge. This two-foot-high jump lay at the entrance to an extremely wide sweeper at last year's Las Vegas supercross, for example. The fastest line is to the inside, but the jump tends to force riders to go wide. It's a complex situation that actually has a rather basic solution, as Honda's Jeremy McGrath demonstrates.

"Normally, you want to hit the face of any jump as straight on as possible; otherwise it will mess you up in the air," McGrath begins. "But since this jump is relatively short, and because it doesn't have any ruts or grooves on the face, you can hit it at an angle to set up for the turn. I take the widest line possible leading into the entrance and then aim toward the inside line in the corner. Your speed should depend on the distance from the jump to the inside of the turn." Notice how McGrath is leaning into the turn just a bit while standing.

"Since you will have to slow down for the turn, you usually shouldn't jump too far," McGrath says. "Try to keep the bike as low as possible, and use your legs and arms to soak up some of the speed on the face of the jump. For better balance, you should also turn your bar out just slightly. The gyroscopic effect helps you gain more control over your bike, but you have to straighten it out before you land. If you land with the bar turned, there's a good chance your front end will wash out."

"Because you need to slow down quickly, you need to land front wheel first," McGrath instructs. "Push down on the handlebar and try to lighten the footpegs. This normally isn't a comfortable position, but it works really well under these circumstances. Had there been a lot of ruts instead of this flat surface, I probably would have landed both wheels at the same time."

"Once the front wheel touches down, you need to pull in the clutch and prepare to start braking," McGrath says. "Stay standing until the suspension rebounds, then use your normal technique for the particular turn, which, in this case, would be sitting. When you land, it's also important to weight the outside peg, otherwise, too much pressure on the inside peg could cause your rear wheel to wash out."

ENDURO

McGRATH ON ACCELERATING OUT OF TURNS

Mastering whoop riding techniques or getting enough nerve to conquer a big double or triple jump are integral steps in the quest toward becoming a better overall racer. Sometimes riders spend far too much time concentrating on them, however, and forget that basic techniques also help put trophies on the mantel.

Proper acceleration is one of those often overlooked skills. After all, it's not glamorous like whipping 'er sideways over a jump or quadrupling into a set of nasty whoops. Here's four-time supercross champ Jeremy McGrath to explain his simple technique—which is all but guaranteed to shave lap times.

1 "No matter if you are beginning your acceleration after landing from a jump or coming out of a turn, it all begins with proper body positioning," McGrath insists. "You want to be set up to accelerate hard in such a way that you won't wheelie but also so your suspension will work."

In this right-hand turn at the Pontiac supercross, McGrath exits perfectly and has his weight forward.

"You have to watch how much throttle you apply, but you want to get on the gas as soon as possible. Remember, if the throttle isn't on, you're not going anywhere."

McGrath also points out that if you apply too much throttle, you could cause the back end to slide out. But if you don't give it enough, you'll lose valuable time and risk getting passed.

In this particular case, he uses a rut to facilitate harder acceleration.

2 Here, unlike in perfectly groomed areas, McGrath found it necessary to center his weight once he began his drive. These acceleration bumps wreak havoc with suspension, which usually makes it difficult to get a good drive when the majority of the weight is carried over the front of the seat.

3 Throughout the entire turn, McGrath weighted the outside footpeg to provide additional traction. Notice that he also leaned forward the entire time (still keeping his posterior centered on the seat) to weight the front end in order to keep the bike from wheeling.

"You should always keep your finger on the clutch in case the front end comes off the ground too much," McGrath adds. "It's usually much better to slip the clutch for a second rather than chop the throttle and have to wait for the engine to build rpm again once you get situated."

ADVANCED RIDING TECHNIQUE

UNDERCUT, BANKED TURNS

This banked turn is actually on Scott Summers's motocross practice track, but it simulates common woods turns quite well. This turn has always been banked, with a sharp transition from flat ground to the bank. But when the bank becomes soft and wet, a deep rut develops at the base—as often happens in the woods. Check out the photos as Summers demonstrates the options for this rut—and the consequences of muffing it.

OPTION 1: Summers first attacked the rut like a motocrosser—fast and aggressive, with both wheels in the rut. The problem is that off-road bikes have somewhat soft suspension that moves around more than motocross suspension does. Because of this, the footpeg sliced off a massive wave of dirt. The dragging fork-leg underhang throws up smaller roost, as well. At the very least, all that dragging scrubs speed off and slows you down.

RESULT 1: One out of three times, Summers could attack the corner moto–style and pull it off by wheelying out. The other two times the front end tucked under, his foot hit the ground and he nearly got sucked off the back of the bike.

OPTION 2: At the beginning of the turn, before the rut gets too deep, Summers steers the front wheel out of the rut and up the bank. Look behind the bike and check out how high the front-wheel tracks go on the bank. You definitely don't want to let the front wheel go over the bank, but by steering out and above the rut, Summers maintains speed, doesn't drag any hard parts and gains necessary leg clearance.

PHOTOS: KAREL KRAMER

HOW TO TACKLE NASTY CORNERS

One of the more challenging obstacles encountered while riding off-road is a corner that has been built up at the base of another obstacle, such as a rock wall. This type of corner psyches out many riders because the penalty for overshooting the turn is severe, much more so than if the rock wall were a bush or even a cactus, for example. This corner at the Laughlin round of the Best in the Desert Silver State Series was surrounded by huge, ankle-snapping, body-scraping, bike-bending rocks. A sandy straightaway leads into the turn, and a rock uphill with a square-edged kicker follows the turn. Entering the turn too hot can force a rider to splatter on the rocks, so setting up for this turn is very important.

This is a perfect example of why you should ride with your head up, constantly scanning the terrain ahead. Here, compare Six Days multimedalist Jeff Fredette's attack on this type of obstacle to that of two other riders. When studying advanced moves in a rocky situation like this, remember that many top riders use foam inserts in their tires. If you use conventional tubes, you'll want to exercise additional care and caution on rock ledges, since a flat usually ruins a race.

1 Here is the lay of the land: A) a sandy corner leading to the rocky uphill, B) the rock face that spells disaster if too much speed is carried into the corner, C) square-edged kicker in the center of the uphill, D) loose dirt exiting the section.

2 Team Green's Jeff Fredette, just exiting the sandy corner, sets up for the rock hill. Note that he's standing centered over the bike with his head up to look for any possible problems that lie ahead. He's gassing it out of the corner to keep up his momentum for the uphill.

3 As Fredette hits the small but sharp square-edged ledge, he moves his body forward to keep his head over the bar and unweight the rear wheel. He accelerates smoothly to keep from loading the rear wheel into the rock ledge any harder than necessary, but hard enough to carry the front wheel easily with his weight forward. He doesn't allow the front wheel to hit the edge of the rock and wash out the front end.

4 As he begins exiting the corner, he assumes his normal riding position. He has just ridden through sand, rock and loose dirt, forcing him to keep prepared for the changes in available traction.

5 Here *Dirt Rider*'s Tom Webb chooses to ride higher on the rock to avoid hitting the angled portion of the square edge. His rear wheel, therefore, is less likely to slide out when it crosses this lip. Webb's body position is further forward and more upright than Fredette's was; he's a taller rider, so his attack position naturally puts his weight further forward.

6 This amateur rider chose to sit down through the same section. That position will subject him to abuse. While seated, he won't be able to maneuver as quickly, and the already loaded suspension won't react as it should. This riding position can end up being a lot more work—especially if you have to pick your bike up off the ground.

PHOTOS: DONNIE BALES

SCOTT SUMMERS ON DOWNHILL RUTS LEADING INTO A TURN

The ISDE will be held in Italy this year in a hard-packed and rocky locale. The hilly ground can also be riddled with ruts. There's a good chance that racers will encounter a section like this one. This downhill ends in a clay, rut turn that would really let you rail, but rain ruts have ruined the potentially good approach. This alternate line and technique proved quite efficacious. It can be applied to any off-camber that leads into a berm, as well.

1 "The main lines leading into this left turn on both the outside and the middle are pretty messed up, and since the ground is hard clay, it'd take a lot of work to run them back in. Even the line that allows the longest acceleration still leaves no room or traction to brake for the turn. Note that the ground gets more off-camber as I approach the turn. That means I must cross any ruts at as close to a right angle as possible."

2 "As I approach the steepening off-camber, I ease off the brakes a little (although I brake all the way into the rut) and straighten the bike for maximum traction. I also get my body into position for the upcoming turn. I know the tires won't hold on a slippery off-camber like this, but that's part of the plan to get smoothly into the rut berm in the corner. I'm looking slightly to the left at the line I'll be hitting."

3 "Now that I'm in the correct riding position for a left turn, I again lean the bike into the turn. As I lean on the off-camber, I steer the front wheel smoothly down into the rut, although there's no way the tires can hold all the way. At the bottom of the frame, you can see the start of the rut berm. At this point, the ruts are gone, so I slide the bike down the off-camber smoothly in the turn with a good, solid berm."

4 "I lift my left foot as the front wheel drops completely into the berm. I don't want that foot to catch on the ground if the front end uses more travel than I think it will. If you look closely, you can see the little sideways roost the tire threw as it slid off the cambered bank. When the rear wheel reaches this point, my braking will naturally slide it down into the rut. Then I'll get on the gas smoothly and get on with the turn."

25

CORNERING: OPEN YOUR EYES!

One of the most common mistakes amateurs make is wasting their prerace practice sessions cutting as many wide-open laps as possible. Watching pros during practice is an educational experience for the eagle-eyed spectator, however. Most pros use their practice sessions to try different lines and experiment with their bikes. Sure, they're also trying to cut some fast laps and get a feel for their equipment, but checking out all of the options on the track is most important.

Take this corner at the Phoenix SX, for example. The 180-degree wide left-hander had a loamy berm on the outside and a deep rut on the extreme inside. The corner followed a section of jumps that, if the riders doubled, catapulted them toward the outside line. Check out the different lines that four of the nation's best riders found.

1 After doubling over the last set of jumps, Honda of Troy's Larry Ward carries his speed into the corner and rides the high line. Ward rides smoothly through the corner, expending a minimal amount of energy.

2 While Suzuki's Greg Albertyn (8) doubles the jumps and follows the same line as Ward did, Yamaha's John Dowd (14) opts to single the jumps and cut to the extreme inside of the corner, where a deep rut lies. In doing so, Dowd sneaks under Albertyn and blocks him while entering the following whoop section.

3 Naturally, railing a rut is more difficult than riding a soft, loamy berm. The only way to make effective use of the inside line is to get through the rut smoothly and quickly. Here, Manchester Honda's Damon Bradshaw gets a little too aggressive in the rut and catches too much traction. Though Bradshaw looks cool as he wheelies out of the rut, it's definitely slower than taking the outside line. When making your line selection, take into account the difficulty. If there's a chance that you'll walk the rut and lose time, go for the outside.

4 While the majority of the riders go for the inside or the outside, Suzuki's Jeremy McGrath opts for a completely different approach. Creative lines have helped catapult McGrath to four consecutive supercross titles. Here, he doubles the jumps but gets on the brakes hard as soon as he lands. He then heads for the middle of the corner—lower than the berm, yet above the rut. McGrath squares off the corner and actually cuts *over* the rut, which gives him an excellent line in the next whoop section. In choosing this line, he makes use of the faster double-jump technique, yet avoids the extra distance of the outside line and the rough rut on the inside.

STEVE HATCH ON TURNS IN TIGHT WOODS

PRO GRIP
ROAD TO
Italy

S oil conditions in the woods often permit the pure perfection of bar-dragging bike lean angles in the soft, deep-loamy-bermed turns. Unfortunately, areas with that type of berms and dirt are usually littered with trees. Sure, you could go for the bar-drag lean, but a tree will certainly tear your head off before you can complete the turn. Since this is a common woods obstacle, we turned to former national enduro champ Steve Hatch to explain how he handles trees in turns. To get a good view for our cameras, we had Hatch demonstrate his technique in this turn on the grass track for Illinois' Moose Run, with plenty of room to miss the tree.

1 "Usually a turn approach this abrupt follows another tree you had to miss. Any tight woods section will have many turns like this with the tree right in the turn entrance, so a motocross style won't work here. As I set up for the turn, I keep my weight centered over the bike, but notice how far up on the bike I'm sitting. I enter the turn hot, because I'll use a brake-slide to get the back wheel started around in the proper direction. Look at my head, my attention is concentrated on the pivot point. If I look *at* the tree, I *will* hit it. I look where I want to go, not where I'm afraid I might go."

2 "As the front wheel passes the tree, I have the rear brake locked and the rear end slides around closer to a proper angle for the rut around the tree. I keep my eyes on the pivot point of the rut, since I haven't changed direction yet. I skim the left end of the handlebar as close to the tree as possible, but I don't hit it. That can knock me off-line or even give my wrists or hands a shock. Notice that my elbows are still well up, and I have my body in the classic attack position."

3 "Now the front wheel rolls smoothly into the rut. I make sure my leg is past the tree, and I use the transition to the turn to tuck my elbow in and miss the tree. The bike and my body are more upright than ideal for a turn entrance, but with a tree on the inside, there's no other way. I make a second transition here. I ease off the brakes and smoothly ease on the throttle and feed out the clutch. A blast of sudden power here could cause lost time or even a spin-out crash."

4 "I pass the tree, and my body position is back to pure moto: centered on the bike, forward on the saddle, elbows up and on the gas. My left foot is almost as far forward as the front of the tire. Notice, too, that my head is now well up so I can look down the trail for any new obstacles. Note that the roost is quite small. I still need to be smooth with the throttle and clutch."

5 "In the midst of the turn, I'm still in attack position but sit a little more upright and lean up in preparation for standing the bike up straight. The roost from the rear tire is so small it almost can't be seen. This turn has a tiny, soft rut, and I don't want to blow it out."

6 "At the turn exit, my foot returns to the left peg, but I still weight the right peg. The roost grows as I use power to straighten up the bike for the following straight."

7 "I use power to bring the rear of the bike around. Now the bike is fairly upright, my weight is completely centered, feet are on the pegs. I lean back slightly for maximum traction. Check out the roost! I want to be wide-open and accelerate as quickly as conditions allow. That's why I train. I don't want to coast; I want to accelerate hard, brake hard and make the most of every second. I only coast to hold a steady speed when forced to!"

CUTTING CORNERS

Cornering is one of the most important skills required to go fast around a motocross course. Good starts and jumping ability are also necessary, but if you can't get in and out of corners quickly, what's the point? Rutted corners are the most tricky and take the most technique. You are also much more likely to fall in a rutted turn.

By Dirt Rider Staff

1 The most important thing when negotiating ruts is to get both of your wheels safely into the rut before starting your turn. You can't blast into a rut with the same amount of speed as you can a loamy, bermed corner. Look at the rut as you enter it and make sure your wheels are in line. Lifting your inside leg serves two purposes: It gets your foot up and out of the way and it allows you to dab in case you lose your balance. Dragging your leg behind the bike in a rut will throw off your balance, and you can go down.

2 Once you're settled into the rut, make sure to look ahead. I look inside the rut to see what's ahead—there may be a rock or big, choppy acceleration bumps. Some people like to look to the inside of the rut to help them stay in it. Never look to the outside of the rut; you go where you look, and the outside is definitely not the hot ticket.

PHOTOS: DIRT RIDER ARCHIVES

3 Some ruts allow you to get on the gas before the actual apex of the corner. You need to be in complete control to get on the gas early, and the rut has to be smooth and deep enough to hold you in. But don't try this in shallow ruts; your back end will probably fly out of the rut, and you'll do a huge doughnut and go down. Apply pressure to the outside footpeg and the side of the bike with your knee and thigh.

4 This rut had some choppy bumps in it. About the only thing you can do is hold on and absorb the impact with your butt. Stay neutral on the bike. I've found leaning forward causes your back end to hop around more than it should and leaning back causes you to get too much traction and wheelie uncontrollably. You also don't want to gas it *too* hard through the choppy acceleration bumps—your back end might bounce out of the rut altogether.

TROUBLESHOOTING

Everyone makes mistakes in ruts—it's unavoidable. If you get into trouble in a rut, don't panic. Stay loose and back off on the throttle; being out of shape in a rut is not corrected by pinning it.

Back wheel on inside: Don't worry too much if your back wheel is on the inside of the rut. Chances are that if you continue your corner, the back end will drop into the rut and get you back in line. Be prepared for this, though—if you're not, you might lose your balance and tip over the high side.

Back wheel on outside: If your back tire didn't get into the rut but your front wheel did, the most important thing to do is go easy on the throttle. If you gas it, your back end will spin out and you'll end up on your butt. You need to use your inside leg to help paddle your way through. At this point, survival is the name of the game.

Front wheel on inside: It's not altogether bad if your front wheel is up on the inside and your rear wheel is in the rut. You may be able to compensate for the odd angle with upper-body positioning, and you may even be able to ride out of the rut altogether on the inside. Throttle control is important because this could also result in a big body.

Front wheel on outside: This is the worst situation to be in, with your front wheel on the outside and back wheel inside. Your front end will probably wash out on the low side and throw you down, but if you react quickly, you may be able to steer away from the rut and ride out of it completely. Then you should look for an outside berm to bank off of.

NO BRAKES

Never drag your brakes through a rut. Doing this will make the bike want to stand upright, and you want the bike to be leaned over in a rut. Get all of your braking done before you enter the rut—the idea is to make the entire corner into one flowing motion.

TO STAND OR SIT?

This all depends on what the braking bumps that precede the rut are like. If they're big and deep, you'll have to stand as you ride through them. When you sit down, you would already be well into the start of the rut. Ideally, you should get on the gas at the same moment that you sit down. This compresses the suspension, lowers the bike and allows you to get cranked over. If there aren't many bumps, it's best to sit down before the rut and enter it in your normal cornering position. This allows you to make the corner into one sweeping motion, which takes less energy and is less risky.

5 Staying loose is very important in ruts. If you get all tense, you'll never flow right through them. Here the acceleration bumps caused me to lose my balance for a split second, but because I was nice and loose, I was able to compensate with my upper body and stay on the gas.

COOPER ON ULTRA-HIGH-SPEED TURNS

Third- and fourth-gear turns always pose an interesting dilemma. Riders must choose between the traditional seated position or standing, which is less common. Just like every other facet of off-road riding, the best method depends on a number of factors. We asked USA's ISDE Trophy Team alternate Guy Cooper to provide some general rules to help you decide which position is best.

In this sequence, Cooper shows us how to blitz through an ultra-high-speed turn with confidence. This 45-degree turn is connected by two really fast straightaways, and the technique incorporates a little roadrace thinking.

PHOTOS: KEN FAUGHT

1 "You almost have to treat high-speed turns like straightaways when it comes to body positioning. If the ground is smooth enough for you to stay seated, then that's probably your best approach. But if there is even one bump that could unsettle your suspension, standing is always best.

"I always look for the most gradual arc so I can maintain my speed; this is something that roadracers do. I enter the turn kind of wide while looking for the smoothest, most bump-free line that offers traction. I also look for a berm that may have developed and can give me something to bank off of."

2 "Once I actually start turning, I slide my weight back so I can counteract any disruptions in the steering. If your front wheel deflects off of a rock or a bump, the bike temporarily slows down, and if your weight is too far forward, you could lose your balance. In extreme instances, you could even go over the bar if the front wheel were to tuck in far enough."

PHOTOS: KEN FAUGHT

3 "Notice that my body position doesn't change through the entire turn. I try to maintain the same positioning until I'm ready to exit the turn. It's also very important to keep your knees and elbows bent. If you lock them into position, you won't be able to assist your bike's suspension when it hits rough terrain."

4 "Upon exiting the turn, I shift my weight forward so I can return to the neutral [or centered] riding position. At this point I'm in a really good location to quickly readjust my bodyweight and position to accommodate the next obstacle."

EMIG ON NEGOTIATING RUTTED TURNS

When riding motocross or supercross there is one sure bet: You will encounter rutted turns. How you attack them will determine if you're having a good or bad day. Rutted turns are probably the hardest sections of a track to go fast through without mak-ing mistakes. If you can master this type of turn, you're a step ahead of your competition. In this "Pro Riding Secrets," AMA National and supercross champion Jeff Emig shows us the fastest way to go through a rutted turn.

1 Emig is hard on the brakes when setting up for the turn. It's important to do most of your braking before rutted turns since they're very bumpy and you do not want your suspension fully compressed in the turn and not in the usable part of the stroke. The setup for the turn is also the moment when Emig picks the line he'll use. His body is in the attack position with his head over the bar and he's looking ahead.

2 Emig lets off the brakes a little here. The suspension starts to come up to absorb any of the bumps in the turn. Still standing and in the attack position, Emig's getting ready to sit down and hit the point that he wants to pivot off. In a right-hand turn you have to brake early because you won't be able to drag your brakes while entering the turn—when you sit down and extend your right foot to avoid the ruts your foot will be off the peg.

3 Emig sits down and leans forward with his foot up to avoid snagging the rut. The rut is deep in this section and you can tell by the spray of dirt that his footpeg is still dragging. While still looking ahead, he settles into the groove and starts to accelerate. Once you have committed to a rut, it's important to follow it throughout the turn.

4 Emig is hard on the gas in the attack position while looking ahead to the next obstacle. He transfers his weight to the middle of the seat and lets the bike drift out just a little. At this point he has cleared the rut and is hard on the gas, powering to the next section of the track.

31

MIKE LAFFERTY ON BRAKE SLIDE TURNS

A few years ago, brake-sliding turns was the way to win in the woods. That's why the Husky Auto was king. Recently, however, emphasis has been on keeping momentum in the turns. Still, there are times when brake-sliding is the best option. Entering tight downhill turns on trails normally ridden in the opposite direction is one scenario begging for brake-sliding because the entrance to this kind of turn is usually wide and the apex and exit of the turn are tight. Follow national enduro champ Mike Lafferty as he handles this turn.

1 "This corner has a steep downhill entrance, but the off-camber is well bermed. The trail originally went the opposite direction, but this year the direction was reversed. In this photo I have swung wide to give myself the best line so I can maximize speed. I have the wheels right out on the edge of the trail, but I'm looking toward the inside of the turn and I'm starting to steer that way. Notice that I have my weight up out of the seat but I am still weighting the front end. I want the rear wheel, not the front wheel, to slide."

2 "Here, the front wheel is aimed toward the very bottom of the berm. The rear wheel is sliding since I have locked up the rear brake while holding the clutch all the way in to allow the engine to keep running. I'm shifting my weight to the outside of the bike, though I have the inside peg weighted. In a brake-slide your hips control the direction of the bike."

3 "The rear wheel has slid around until it's on the face of the berm. I've let out the clutch and taken my foot off the brake at the same time and am accelerating smoothly away. If I got too sudden with the clutch or the throttle at this point, the rear wheel could lose traction and go over the side of the berm. At best I'd lose time, at worst I would highside down the hill into the bushes. It's also imperative to preserve shoulder health by not skidding the front wheel. I have it up on the wall of the berm and my body position is so far forward that I'm actually ahead of the seat. I'm not completely seated here, but if I were, I'd be sitting on the tank. I'm in the perfect position to accelerate out of this berm as hard as possible."

32

We've heard it over and over again: "Never follow another rider, always try to pick your own line if possible." We all know it, but we still make mistakes and trail a rider into rutted lines because it's the fastest way around the track. What happens? The guy in front goes down, you get stuck behind him and five riders go around.

Most of the time this is avoidable, but a turn may have a blind corner and, before you know it, some guy is laid out in your line. The key to preventing this is to think before you make an evasive action. If you make a sudden move, there's a good chance you too will stall or crash.

Here, Mike LaRocco encounters a downhill off-camber turn with hay bales blocking the view of the entire turn. LaRocco has already committed to the rut before he realizes Lance Smail is down.

The key to attacking any section, motocross or off-road, is too look ahead. There are many cases where a rider can avoid a problem by discovering it before it happens. Especially in motocross, a rider can lose one to five positions in a split second if a downed rider is in his line. In this photo (top), LaRocco is looking ahead and picking the fastest line in the tough off-camber turn. Because of how the turn is set up, there is no visibility to the bottom of the turn. When LaRocco picks his line, he has no idea Smail is on the ground.

As soon as LaRocco sees the apex of the turn, he realizes there is a rider down. LaRocco gets hard on the brakes to avoid making contact with Smail. LaRocco has two options at this time, foot plant and try to go above Smail or jump the berm and go below him. Because the turn is on an off-camber, it would take LaRocco a lot of time to go above Smail. There is also a good chance he will tangle with Smail, who is trying to pick up his bike. LaRocco has to be careful; if he tries to steer out of the rut, he could easily high side and go down himself. At this point, LaRocco has scrubbed off his momentum and planned his next action. He straightens up the bike slightly and applies power to the rear wheel by popping the clutch. Putting power to the ground lightens the front wheel and makes it easier to drive over the rut. Once the front wheel is over the berm, the rear wheel will follow.

pro riding secrets

PRS

Because LaRocco is always looking forward, he picks the best alternate line and motors off. As you can see, LaRocco is well on his way before Smail even gets back on his bike. According to LaRocco, it is best to avoid situations that require evasive moves, but you must be able to take on any situation at a moment's notice. Because LaRocco made a clean line change, there was little chance he would lose position or time.

STEVE HATCH

SAVE

ENERGY: KEEP YOUR FEET ON THE PEGS

BY MARK KARIYA

I think there's kind of a misconception where everybody believes they have to have a foot out for balance [in turns]," Suzuki's Steve Hatch says.

"You really don't."

Say what? Not all of us are trials riders or AA racers possessing the balance of high-wire artists, after all.

Granted, Hatch admits that "higher-speed corners or sweepers where there's nothing to pivot or turn on, it's probably a good idea [to have your inside foot thrust out and forward]."

But in most trail situations, the turns are tighter and there's often a small rut you can take advantage of—so why not take advantage? Hatch believes that keeping your feet on the pegs has many benefits, chief among them the energy savings and less disruption of body positioning (resulting in less effect on the motorcycle's equilibrium).

"A lot of times in off-road when it's so tight and technical, I kind of developed this form from being so far up on the bike to help put more weight on the front end," he says. "When you put your foot out, even if you're really strong, it's hard to keep as far forward [on the bike]; you kind of slide back to the middle of the seat.

"With your feet [on the pegs], you can grip [the tank with your knees] and put your body weight an extra inch or two forward, and that helps tenfold: The more you can weight that front wheel, the more you can turn on a dime—and it saves energy. If you figure you don't have to put your foot out 10,000 times in an eight-hour enduro race or 5000 times in a GNCC, it keeps your body weight correct, it keeps your arms up and it keeps more weight on the front wheel. I've taught a lot of people that, and they say they can't believe how much energy it saves.

"And it doesn't upset the bike, too. That's another thing that not many people think about. When you have a bike and you're stationary on it, then you throw something off it [like your foot], it weights [the bike differently]. Then to pull [the foot] back up weights it [differently] also."

Here, Steve Hatch zips through the turn as a motocrosser would typically do it: body as far forward as possible, foot extended near the front axle and elbows up. Take a close look at the position of the bike in relation to the rut, though: The bike is actually perpendicular to the rut's surface, isn't it? That means the bike's weight is transmitted directly downward, providing a surprising amount of traction—which means sticking that foot out isn't really necessary because the chances of the tires sliding are markedly reduced.

Same turn, nearly the same place in the turn, yet Hatch has his feet on the pegs. Other than getting smacked in the face with that branch, he's got no worries, is going just as fast yet is expending less energy than the previous shot. Take advantage of those little ruts, and you'll be fresher at the finish.

TAKING ON FLAT, SLICK CORNERS

Have you ever wondered how top riders can go so fast? It's not because their bikes are so much quicker than the competition's; it's because they corner so much better. Some of the most difficult corners to negotiate are flat, slick turns without a berm or groove. Oftentimes a rider is either too timid entering the turn or he goes in too hot and ends up drifting wide, opening up the inside line for a pass. The key is to find traction, forcing the bike to bite the slick surface below. Top supercross riders have mastered this method of attack so we had Jeremy McGrath demonstrate the perfect technique.

PHOTOS: DONNIE BALES

1 MC starts to enter the turn on the gas and in the attack position—arms up, leaning forward with his head over the bar. He has also shifted his body to the right side of the seat to prepare for the turn. His foot is off the peg and kept slightly above the ground. If the ground is broken up with holes and curbs, keep your extended leg forward to avoid snagging your boot in a hole. Catching a boot can snap your leg back and throw off your timing going into a turn or even break your leg.

2 In this shot, McGrath has rolled off the throttle and picked a line around the turn. You don't want to snap the throttle off rapidly, just roll it at a steady rate. When you snap the throttle off, it causes the rear wheel to lose its bite on the ground and start to slide out. If you look closely, you can see McGrath does not use his brakes to take on this turn. Tighter turns may require braking, but be sure to apply smooth, even pressure. A little too much front or rear brake will put you on the ground in a heartbeat. He lets the bike float into the turn and uses his body position to force the bike to maintain traction.

3 As he enters the apex of the turn, MC leans the bike in even further while trying to keep his body perpendicular to the ground. Notice his butt is completely rotated to the side of the seat as he applies pressure to the right footpeg to maintain maximum traction. Right past this point, McGrath starts to roll on the power and prepare for the next obstacle.

4 With the turn pretty much behind him, McGrath rotates his body position back to the center of the bike while feeding more power to the ground. Because there's a jump following the turn, he has to position his bike almost upright before the face. Traction is also key at this point. Although McGrath wants to put as much power to the ground as possible, he does not want the rear wheel to spin under him. It's a good idea to keep at least one finger on the clutch to regulate the power delivery if necessary. You want to ensure that the bike does not slide into the face of the jump. If the bike is still sliding, it can easily cause you to high side when the suspension releases on the face of the jump. Find a slick corner as in our demonstration and work on improving your speed through the section.

STICKING

JEREMY McGRATH AND RICKY CARMICHAEL

FLAT CORNERS WITH JUMPS

BY SCOTT HOFFMAN

Becoming a better rider is more complicated than just learning to twist the throttle. It is a matter of throttle control. In this tip we are going to explain how to maximize throttle control and body positioning on flat corners. Imagine shaving a split second off each turn; by the end of each lap that time could add up to a second, and by the end of the race it could make the difference between winning and losing. It's not often that the average moto track would have a technical section like the one we have shown, although tracks do lay out single jumps right out of corners and jumps going into corners.

1 While studying the track, Jeremy McGrath discovers that landing his bike on the inside will give him the best and the straightest line going into the turn. MC is also memorizing several alternative lines in the event he is trying to make a pass or a rider has gone down in the main line. This is where looking ahead will pay off, if you are aware of an incident well enough in advance, there is time to change lines.

2 Without a specific rut or line to set his bike in, McGrath has to find traction on the flat surface. Here, MC is on the pegs with his weight slightly over the bar to maintain a consistent weight bias from front to back. This is also where throttle control is critical; he applies a slight amount of power to the rear wheel to maintain a drive but without spinning the rear tire or sliding out. On the other hand, coasting the bike around the turn makes it very difficult for a rider to find traction and the bike will want to stand up. Weighting the outside peg while keeping the tires on a consistent edge helps maintain traction.

3 In this shot, Ricky Carmichael is using the same line but he sits down to add that extra bite to the ground. The technique is the same, but Carmichael feels he could carry more speed through the turn sitting down. If the ground was slightly more tacky, RC may have preferred to stand.

4 With the jump right after the apex of the turn, McGrath will use the seat-bounce technique to get the lift to clear the next obstacle. Because of the approach, throttle and clutch control are essential. Even if the jump after the turn was not in the picture, the drive out of the corner is equally important. MC rolls on the throttle fairly rapidly while slipping the clutch at the same time. When McGrath feels his bike is hooking up at the base of the jump, he snaps the throttle to the stops and releases the clutch completely to get the maximum drive. All of this would not have been possible if he had ridden too aggressively and spun the rear tire or the drive through the turn was too slow. There is a fine line between too fast and too slow, but being able to find the zone is what makes a better rider. Go out, pick a turn and keep hitting the turn until you too can find the difference between too slow and too fast.

ROOT AVOIDANCE 101

"Roots are one of the scariest obstacles in the woods. They are slippery, and they pound your suspension and body. Most importantly, they can throw you onto the ground quicker than anything. I inspect a course closely for roots while walking it. If there is a way that I can avoid riding across slippery roots, I'll take it—even if it means using more energy.

1 "These nasty roots are on a slippery uphill, right out of a tight turn. I could ride across them, but I'd have to almost coast to maintain control. They not only have a -10 traction coefficient, they stick up high enough to washboard the rear suspension. I noticed two things while walking: The first root is a fairly abrupt obstacle, but it lies straight across the trail; the last root is radically angled across the trail. If the first root were angled, I'd never attempt to jump it. I would have wheelied into it, then unloaded the suspension and coasted across."

2 "I have to be totally on when I exit the rutted turn before the straight. I need to pick up all the speed I can and get into my standing attack position as soon as possible. I aim for the portion of root that looks like it lies perpendicular to the trail. I load the suspension, then coordinate the clutch and throttle to give me maximum acceleration as the suspension rebounds from hitting the root. The front wheel has already launched off the root here, and I am still loading the rear end into the root."

3 "I radically exaggerate getting light on the pegs and bend my legs to let the bike rise up as easily as possible. I also attempt to correct for the bike's sliding on the root a bit on take-off with some body English while I am in the air. So far, I am using energy like crazy."

4 "My goal here is to get the front wheel over the angled root. Any of the other roots would bounce me around and cause wild wheelspin, but that angled one could throw me onto the ground! I want a front-wheel landing for two reasons: One, it might let the rear wheel stay in the air long enough to clear the root; two, if I don't clear it with the rear wheel, I want the front wheel on the ground for control."

5 "The instant that the rear wheel is over the root, I am back in my preferred riding position: centered and balanced, with my head over the triple clamps. This area after the roots has the best traction on this little straight, so I want to be ready to gain speed and cut seconds from this section. I used a lot of energy, but I got through the section safely and fast!"

PHOTOS: KAREL KRAMER

Jumps

CHAPTER THREE

Steve Lamson: How to attack uphill jumps 39
Ryan Hughes: Conquering tiered uphill doubles 40
McGrath on taming uneven whoops .41
Lamson on not doing doubles 42
When you don't clear that double 43
How Steve Lamson handles jumps with kicker lips 44
Jeff Emig on tackling rutted jumps 45
Ty Davis tells when it's best to roll, not jump 46
Jeff Emig on front-wheel landings 47
Downhill doubles with John Dowd 48
Flying low by Jeremy McGrath 49
Kevin Windham on making the inside line 50
Michael Craig on seat-bounce jumping 51
Larry Ward on skipping across obstacles 52
Soaking up small jumps with Tallon Vohland 53
Anatomy of the perfect jump with Nathan Ramsey 54
Airing out off-road with Ty Davis 56
Drop-Offs with Kevin Windham 57

STEVE LAMSON
HOW TO ATTACK UPHILL JUMPS

The general nature of an uphill robs tremendous amounts of momentum from any machine as the engine gets bogged down under a load. Maintaining speed becomes increasingly more difficult when traction goes away. This has never been more apparent than when watching small-bore pilot Steve Lamson negotiate this uphill jump in Slovakia during this year's Motocross des Nations. The newly crowned AMA 125cc National Champ, however, put his technique to the test and we captured it on film to break it down into the various steps. Here's how it's done:

1 "In reality, most of your speed is determined at the base of the hill," Lamson begins. "It's very important that you get the best possible drive, otherwise you'll never be able to get up to your maximum speed. Regardless of how slow or fast you attack the hill, you should keep your weight centered and stand up, especially if it's rough. Most importantly, never back out of the throttle because you'll lose engine rpm quickly. If you need to decelerate for some reason, like to keep the front end from wheeling, then just slip the clutch a little."

2 "In the previous photo I attacked the face of the jump just like I would any other high-speed jump. Notice, however, that as I start to take off, I shift my weight to the furthermost portion of the seat," Lamson continues. "The idea is to keep the bike parallel with the ground during takeoff."

3 "About midflight I quickly move my weight forward in one motion," Lamson says. "This motion helps lower the force of the bike to the ground quicker than if I were to stay seated near the rear fender."

4 "Because the front end is still too light and because I've lost too much momentum, I can tell that I would loop out if I were to instantly land in the normal attack position," Lamson observes. "Therefore, I stay standing momentarily but now have most of my weight over the tank."

5 "It's only after I'm totally confident that I can keep the front end on the ground will I slowly slide back on the seat," Lamson explains. "All of the body motion I described is just a way to keep the bike as low to the ground as possible while maintaining the delicate balance between enough and too much traction."

RYAN HUGHES
CONQUERING TIERED UPHILL DOUBLES

One of the most fun double jumps is the tiered jump because it allows big air without a harsh landing. After takeoff, the bike floats in the air and then, when done properly, lands smoothly after gaining elevation.

Another bonus is that the penalty for landing short on tiered jumps is generally not as severe as on traditional doubles. Usually, if you can just get the front wheel on top of the second jump, you're in pretty good shape.

This year's Motocross des Nations course in Slovakia had just such a jump. It lofted riders 15 feet into the air over a distance of 50 feet. Here is Team USA's Ryan Hughes to explain.

1 "I approach the jump in a neutral position with the throttle on," Hughes begins. "This type of double is usually easy to gauge distance on since you can see the second ridge. Also, if you're unclear how much speed is required, remember that it's always easier and safer to overjump this type of obstacle than underjump."

2 "The natural tendency of a bike accelerating all the way off the face of an uphill jump is to launch the front wheel high," Hughes explains. "To offset this, I stay standing with my knees bent and my butt over the center of the seat, but I move my head over the handlebar."

3 "Once in the air, I stand fully erect and begin looking at the next obstacle, which, in this case, is a left-hand turn," Hughes adds. "Notice that I'm still standing, my knees are slightly bent and the bike is nearly level with the landing zone."

4 "As you can clearly see, I have overjumped the second jump slightly but have nothing to worry about," Hughes states. "My objective is to land with the throttle on and keep my weight centered, maybe leaning a little towards the front, to keep the bike from wheelying. Usually, the landings are very smooth and you don't have to worry about a harsh landing that would normally be associated with catching this much air."

McGRATH ON TAMING UNEVEN WHOOPS

Whoop sections are one of the least understood obstacles, and, therefore, the techniques used to master them vary wildly. Take uneven whoops, for example. One of the latest tricks track builders are utilizing is putting one large whoop in the middle of a normal whoop section to break up the timing. Honda's Jeremy McGrath has developed an advanced technique that produces excellent results on this type of obstacle, as he has for most other man-made obstacles found in supercross racing.

1 "Getting a good drive is the most important aspect," McGrath begins. "If you can't build speed quickly enough, then this technique of double jumping onto the bigger whoop won't work. You have to be able to drive off the face and use it like a pre-jump. You really have to drive with the throttle on instead of skimming over the top of it." Notice how McGrath's head is way over the front of the handlebar and his legs are straight. "You want to let the motor and the suspension do all of the work. You can see that my back end is almost bottomed, which is good because once the shock rebounds, it will provide lift."

2 "You have to be careful not to pull up on the handlebar," McGrath instructs. "Pulling up causes the rear wheel to lower because the bike will actually pivot at the footpegs. I usually try to achieve the right body positioning that will allow the bike to jump level, and this can only be accomplished with a lot of practice. If you compare this photo to the previous one, you can see the most crucial part of the trick. I actually let the bike accelerate with as little of my weight as possible. This becomes more clear if you notice that my butt is *still* over the whoop while the bike is way out in front. This is why my body positioning has changed so much." Notice how McGrath's weight is hanging off the bike, his knees are now bent, and his head is over the seat/tank juncture.

3 "I try to maintain the body positioning as long as possible, at least until the rear wheel makes contact with the bigger whoop," McGrath explains. "Any movement on the bike at this point will cause the attitude to change, which could cause one of your wheels to clip."

4 "As the front wheel touches the top of the whoop, I quickly center my weight," McGrath continues. "This particular whoop is like a small tabletop, and I actually have to brake once both wheels touch."

5 "Once you get on top of the jump, you have to be prepared for the next obstacles," McGrath adds. "If it's more whoops, you may consider doubling or tripling into them if you feel it's safe."

LAMSON ON NOT DOING DOUBLES

When you think of defending AMA 125cc National MX Champ Steve Lamson, you think of the one guy in the class that is going to be jumping *all* the doubles. At the Glen Helen National, there was an uphill double right out of a turn and before another turn. The landing was pretty safe, and there was no way to overshoot the next turn since the berm was an entire hillside. Square-edged ledges before the takeoff posed the major problem. If your suspension handled them perfectly, you could clear the jump, but if you hit the bumps wrong, they robbed momentum, forcing you to case the jump. No riders fell, but casing it took a toll on energy in the heat and smog. As the race progressed, it became obvious that the fastest riders were not attempting the jump but choosing a more conservative approach. The riders from 10th back were all jumping it. Check out the photos of second-moto winner Lamson in this section.

1 Lamson carries good speed over the first jump but takes no chances berserking the bumps before the jump. Instead of unloading the suspension to gain elevation, he lets the bike come up to him to kill the lift.

2 Next he pushes the bike down to get back onto the ground sooner. His body positioning is extremely rearward at this point— very bad for landing.

3 Lamson makes absolutely certain to have his body centered over the bike before the landing. That lets the bike absorb the shock of the landing while causing him to expend as little energy as possible. He has timed his landing for the flat area in the middle of the jump. The upslope would cause an abrupt landing that he wants to avoid.

4 The last photo shows that Lamson's factory CR125R's suspension has rebounded, readying the chassis to grab the nearest inside line, make the direction change and head for the next jump. Lamson has wisely resisted the impulse to jump a jump just because it's there. He seeks out lines that allow him to go the fastest while conserving the most energy. He thinks and rides like a champion.

42

PHOTOS: KAREL KRAMER

WHEN YOU DON'T CLEAR THAT DOUBLE

As track builders and promoters work to make tracks safer and suspension technology grows more sophisticated, we see more and more doubles that you "work up to" by simply jumping as far as you can and taking the abuse of the landing. On a rounded second jump, this is a safe and viable plan for improving your jumping technique. Keeping it safe requires that you use proper body positioning to absorb the landing without losing control.

The National at Glen Helen Raceway Park featured a double out of a turn with a very choppy, rough approach. The riders literally did not know whether they could clear the jump or not until they were already in the air. Amateur riders tend to react badly when faced with a hard landing. They push away from the landing, get their weight back as far as their arms will let them and fearfully watch the jump happen to them. These are exactly the wrong reactions. Keeping your weight centered over the bike allows you to use your skeleton and musculature for support upon impact. You also need to keep some bend in your arms and legs at all times. That neutral body stance lets your bike's suspension work its best and affords you the most control over your bike. Check out several riders as they attempted this landing.

1 In the first photo, Ezra Lusk and John Dowd pick drastically different lines over this jump. Lusk is just getting back into his forward and neutral position after going for maximum lift on the takeoff. Dowd has chosen not to double, and his suspension is showing the effects of not having a jump downslope to land upon.

2 Here is Lusk in the air again. He is heading for a very hard landing, but he does not have his weight back. On the contrary, he is upright, forward, and has a slight bend in his knees and elbows to absorb the landing that will come as surely as death and taxes (not in that particular order, hopefully).

3 Casey Johnson has not quite cleared this jump and will land atop the second mound with a very solid thump. He exhibits the exaggerated forward positioning that will allow him to take the impact without the bike's taking a bad bounce. This posture will allow him to stay on the throttle and keep hauling the mail.

4 Mickael Pichon illustrates another view of the proper body position for a safe landing. If the bike were to kick or swap upon landing, you want your weight in the center of the bike. That way, the bike will tend to return to center. It is a definite and difficult mental to decision to get forward, stay forward and stay on the throttle when fear sets in, but you can learn this. All the top riders have, and it will make you faster and safer.

HOW STEVE LAMSON HANDLES JUMPS WITH KICKER LIPS

For most riders, straightforward and uncomplicated jumps are thrilling enough. Add a dug-out kicker lip to the top of any jump, and the thrill and danger factors soar. We picked Team Honda's Steve Lamson's brain for ways to ease the mental strain and potential pain of these jumps.

1 The jump in question is a Mammoth Mountain leap that's constructed of sandy soil. It gets an ugly lip at the crest. Less-aggressive riders ride up the face and shut off, then gas it as they leave the top of the jump. They use the throttle, rather than body position, to control the bike's attitude in the air. In the process, a lip gets dug into the top of the jump. That makes it harder for the amateurs, but the pros (like Lamson) scarcely notice the obstacle. Here's why.

2 Lamson explained that his first choice would be to miss the kicker entirely, if possible. This jump still has a good, smooth line all the way up and off the face on the far left. "Lamy" usually takes the time to get to that side off the jump and avoid problems with a kicker lip. During a race, getting to the best line isn't always the best option, however.

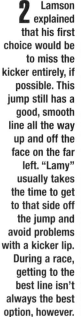

3 When he is forced to the middle of the jump by either the necessity for speed or other riders' interference on the track, Lamson approaches the jump face with good speed in a gear that allows plenty of acceleration. As the suspension compresses on the jump face, Lamson squats into the downward movement of the machine to emphasize the suspension's natural movement.

4 As the suspension rebounds, Lamson extends his body rapidly to exaggerate the lift of the bike. He grips the bike tightly with his legs and goes to full-leg and nearly full-arm extension. Note that he stays centered over the bike in a firm attack position. In this photo, the front wheel has already left the ground; the rear will follow suit as soon as the rear suspension rebounds fully.

5 As the bike leaves the jump-face, Lamson lets the bike come up to him. The jump face here is not overly steep, so he has jumped all the way off the pegs in an effort to let the bike rise as high as possible. The front wheel cleared the kicker easily, but he obviously needed all the lift he could find to let the rear wheel clear it, too. He is now cleanly over the jump, with no chance of losing control, and the rear wheel kept driving for the longest possible time. Making this kind of smooth time on each jump wins races and keeps the rider safe.

PHOTOS: KAREL KRAMER

JEFF EMIG ON TACKLING RUTTED JUMPS

Lots of riders freeze when the track turns rutted—and with good reason: It takes the precision of a brain surgeon to maintain speed in a rut: Any twitch or wobble means the rut will grab your front wheel and try to shake you off the bike.

That, of course, is something most riders try to avoid.

When the ruts lead to a jump, it signals *super*slo-mo to the majority of guys because the last thing you want to do is get spit off on the approach to, or take-off from, a jump.

Kawasaki's Jeff Emig rarely lets ruts shake him up, though, and he gladly shared his secrets on tackling fearsome, rutted jumps.

1 "When racing on tracks with jumps that are very rutted, the first thing to look for is a rut that's shallow and in a good position for the [approach to] the jump," Emig begins. "It's important to look ahead." That can't be stressed enough, especially when it comes to ruts. You *have* to look far ahead, preferably at the jump itself, because if you look down at the rut in front of you, you tend to overcorrect. Naturally, you want to be on the pegs in a crouch, fairly centered over the bike. Notice that Emig puts the balls of his feet onto the pegs. That helps keep the toes up and away from danger, like getting sucked underneath the pegs should the rut get real deep.

2 "When the bike drops into the rut, hit the throttle. Keep your body in the middle of the bike." Again, note how Emig's feet remain parallel to the ground as the bike sinks. This is not the time to have your toes pointed down.

3 "It's important to make sure that the footpegs don't drag," Emig points out. "That's why choosing a shallow groove is so important. An advanced-rider's tip would be to choose a groove that will not launch [you] up but forward for better lap times. So, have fun racing in the ruts, enjoy the challenge and good luck!"

PHOTOS: KEN FAUGHT

TY DAVIS TELLS WHEN IT'S BEST TO ROLL, NOT JUMP

As a former supercross champ, you'd think that Team Green's Ty Davis would jump everything on the trail. He does—unless going for air would slow him down or add undue risk.

Despite what you might think, motocrossers *do* use their heads. In the woods you've got to, of course, or else you'll no doubt end up on yours.

Though everyone agrees that looking well ahead on the trail is important for maintaining speed safely, there will still be times when something catches you by surprise. Referring to a dip on the trail in the Sam Houston National Forest in Texas, Davis admits: "It came up on me too quick, and I didn't see it in time. [Sometimes] you're going through the woods thinking about cornering, cornering. All of a sudden, boom! There's a ditch. Uh oh, now you *have* to ride through it. There are many obstacles that I don't jump the first time over a trail. I never jump blind." Here's how Davis handles it.

1 "I come down the trail in the attack position, with my knees bent," Davis begins. In other words, he's doing nothing out of the ordinary.

2 At the last minute, however, he sees a dip in the trail, catching him a bit off guard. He slows upon seeing it "…to see how bad the ditch is, and determine whether or not to go slower or keep my momentum."

3 "As I ride through it, I accelerate and try to keep the front end light. I try to ride down [into the dip] so I don't slam my front end into [the far side]."

4 As the bike starts out of the dip, Davis shifts his weight forward. He appears more radically forward than he actually is because the bike is beginning to head uphill. "I kind of extend my legs and get back into the hunched [attack] position as soon as possible. As I'm going through it, I try to keep my helmet and the main part of my body in a constant position [relative to the terrain] so I can concentrate on what lies ahead. I don't want my head bobbing up and down too much."

PHOTOS: MARK KARIYA

JEFF EMIG ON FRONT-WHEEL LANDINGS

Almost every motocross track in existence has at least one table-top or double jump—even the most traditional outdoor courses. On these types of jumps, adjusting the attitude of your motorcycle in the air and landing front wheel first is advantageous. Doing so not only smoothes out the landing, but allows you to get back on the gas quicker. Here's reigning 250cc National Champion Jeff Emig to explain the basics of this technique.

2 "As you compress the suspension on the face of the jump, you want to lean forward a bit. Notice that I'm not leaning backward in this photo. I'm letting the front end come up to me. Keeping your upper body slightly forward will automatically begin the nose-down process."

3 "Try to make a smooth arc out of the whole jump. If you can tell from your take-off that the bike isn't gonna nose down on its own, sure, you can use the rear brake. As a matter of fact, you should be ready to, just in case. Anyway, as the bike takes to the air, you should begin to lean even further forward."

1 "The most important thing when trying to nose down your bike while in the air is to have confidence in the bike," Emig says. "Back in the '80s, it was the cool thing to lock up your rear brake in the air, bringing your front end down. Though that's an easy technique to learn, it's not necessarily the best. It's better to get the bike to land front wheel first with body English. When you slam on the rear brake in the air, it stops the rear wheel and lowers the front end, but it also means you'll have to get the rear wheel moving all over again once you land. If you nose down with body English and land with the rear wheel still spinning, you'll be able to accelerate faster. As you approach the jump, you should maintain a neutral body position. Compress the suspension into the face, don't try to suck up the impact with your legs."

4 "Once the bike begins to nose down, relax and let it go. At first, some beginners may panic and worry about endoing. Get used to landing on your front wheel over a smaller jump first, maybe even on flat ground. Chopping your throttle in the air also helps get the front end down."

5 "Landing with your front wheel first—landing with your bike at the same level as the downside of the landing ramp—is a lot smoother," Emig says. "It will not only cut your lap times, it'll help you save a little energy, too.

"Take it slow while perfecting this technique. If you feel you're getting too nose-low, you can pin the throttle and the G-forces from the spinning rear wheel will help bring the front end back up. That's the opposite principle of bringing the front end down by slamming on the rear brake."

DOWNHILL DOUBLES WITH JOHN DOWD

Jumping is a technique that can never be covered enough. Think about it—when you arrive at a track, the first thing you usually do is check out the jumps. Jumping is probably one of the most important techniques that you need to learn in order to go fast. If you can't jump well, chances are you'll be passed by someone who can. Jumping requires a variety of skills—balance, throttle control, brake and clutch control.

There are many types of jumps, but some of the trickiest are blind downhill doubles, like the peristyle jump at the Los Angeles Coliseum SX. The double is 65 feet long, but unlike most downhill doubles, the face of the jump is nonexistent. Instead, riders must double off a drop-off. Here, Team Yamaha's John Dowd shows us the proper technique.

But remember—jumping above and beyond your capabilities is dangerous and can lead to serious injury.

1 Preceding the jump is a left-hand corner. Dowd makes sure that he's in complete control while exiting the corner. Note that he is in the attack position—his body is low and his head is over the handlebar.

2 When you hit the face of a normal jump, the suspension compresses and the rebound helps you gain the necessary altitude. This jump, however, had no face. Here, Dowd prepares to extend his arms and legs as soon as the bike drops away. Because there is no "up," Dowd doesn't need to gas it to clear the second jump. Drop-offs like this can be deceiving because they do not require as much speed as a lipped jump to gain the same amount of distance.

3 Here, Dowd maintains a neutral body position on the bike. Throttle and brake control are very important on a jump like this, especially since it will simply drop you out of the sky (you're not flying through the air in the normal arc). On this jump, Dowd must maintain a relatively level bike position, so it's important that he is comfortable.

4 As Dowd lands, notice that both of his wheels touched down at the same time. This allows him to get back on the gas quickly, without losing any precious time. Dowd is upright on the bike and is bracing himself for the landing. As you can see, the YZ's suspension is fully compressed, which makes proper foot positioning on the pegs important. Dowd is using his legs as a secondary suspension component. Notice that his head is up and he is already eyeing the next obstacle.

FLYING LOW

By Jeremy McGrath

Throughout my career, staying low over jumps has been a big part of my success. I developed this technique during my early days as a BMX racer. Anyway, everyone knows there's no traction in the air, and the faster you can get back onto the ground and on the gas, the faster you'll be. This downhill double is on my natural-terrain track. A lot of guys who ride with me fly much higher than I do over this jump—they don't know my secret.

1 As I approach the jump, I prepare myself to compress the bike's suspension into the face. You want to compress the bike into the face of the jump and time it so the suspension begins to rebound at the same time the bike is leaving the jump face. To compress, I use my arms and my legs, but most of the power comes from my legs.

2 As the suspension unloads and the bike leaves the face of the jump, I suck up the upward momentum of the bike with my body. If you leave the jump face with your arms and legs stiff, you'll fly superhigh, especially after compressing the bike into the face of the jump.

3 Stay loose and relaxed while using this technique. Basically, you want to use your arms and legs to keep the bike from flying high. Let the bike float up toward you, don't let it push your body higher. I've learned over the years that the faster you hit the face of a jump, the lower you can fly. This takes a lot of practice, though. Don't try this for the first time on a huge triple jump with the throttle pinned!

4 In midair, I maintain a neutral body position. Notice how relaxed I look in the air at the peak of the jump. Check out my right boot. I've developed this technique over the years: I let my right foot float off the footpeg, then I hook my heel under the right sidepanel, next to the subframe, and lift up. This causes the front end to dive.

5 A lot of riders use the rear brake to get the front end to dive. I only use that technique in an emergency. It's best to learn how to maneuver the bike's altitude with throttle control and body positioning. To get ready for landing, I move my weight forward.

6 I apply the throttle hard, right at the moment my rear wheel touches down. Lead the bike with your upper body—check out how I'm leaning over the front of the bike. It may not seem like a lot, but little things like that add up when you're maintaining forward momentum. Landing with the gas on will also help prevent your rear suspension from rebounding too quickly and bouncing your back tire off the ground. At this point, I'm already focusing on the next obstacle. Go try it!

PHOTOS: DIRT RIDER ARCHIVES

KEVIN WINDHAM ON MAKING THE INSIDE LINE

Choosing the correct line is a key factor between winning and losing. Kevin Windham, West Coast 125cc Supercross champ, is a tactician when choosing the fastest way around the track. It doesn't matter if you ride supercross or outdoor motocross, the following techniques apply. Oftentimes, tracks have turns right after tabletops or double jumps; there are two ways to attack these sections. After the landing you can drift to the outside and hit a berm to accelerate out of the section. But the shortest distance between two points is a straight line, and this is where Windham struts his stuff. Hitting the inside line is by far the fastest way to approach this section. Windham demonstrates his technique.

1 Before Windham hits the face of the first jump he knows exactly where he wants to land his bike to make the turn. Knowing the turn is right after the landing, Windham wants to land the bike slightly on the outside of the jump to reduce the angle of the turn. In the air, he's already starting to turn the bike to set up for the turn. It is critical to land the bike front wheel first. If the front end is too high, adjust your weight or tap the rear brake to start to bring the front end down.

2 Windham is about to land and he already has his sights set on the turn. Here the bike is slightly angled toward the turn, and he'll land on the downslope of the jump. Be sure not to land with too much of an angle on the bike because the front end might wash out upon landing. As you can see, his weight is slightly back and he has a finger on the clutch for instant traction control.

3 Windham has already committed to the turn and is able to maintain traction into it by weighting the outside peg and keeping his weight over the bar. Body position is critical on flat corners, and Windham prefers to stand throughout the turn in order to prepare for the next jump. Once you've reached the apex of the turn, you can start to power out of it. Throttle and clutch control must be precise because if you apply too much power to the ground the rear tire could spin and you risk the chance of sliding out.

4 After successfully making the inside line, Windham is on the gas and powering off the next jump. As you can see, he has maintained his body position throughout the entire section for traction and bike control. Taking the inside line is a little more difficult, but worth it. In a race, the inside line is a great place to set up for a pass or to fend off a competitor's pass attempts. You can see the advantages of taking the inside following a jump. If you're going to practice this, start on small jumps and work your way up. **M!**

MIKE CRAIG ON SMALL SEAT-BOUNCE JUMPS

In recent years, the seat-bounce jumping technique has become a necessary skill for supercross riders. The tight layout of modern SX tracks requires riders to gain the extra lift produced when hitting the face of a jump while sitting down. Most supercross jump faces are at least as tall as the bike's wheelbase, and the seat-bounce technique is relatively safe.

Smaller jumps, however, are a different story. Because the jump faces are shorter than the bike's wheelbase, extra caution and a slightly revised technique are necessary to properly execute a seat-bounce jump. Here's Honda of Troy's Mike Craig to explain his technique on this relatively small take off jump.

1 "I always try to seat-bounce stuff that's right out of a corner or going right into a corner," Craig said. "In this case, there was time to stand up after the corner, but that increases the chances of having the rear wheel break loose. If you stay seated, you maintain better control of the bike."

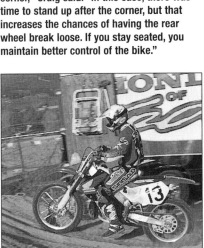

2 "I like to drag my foot in corners," Craig added. "I leave it off the peg for balance and to save myself in case the bike starts to slide or something. When you seat-bounce a jump, it doesn't really matter if your foot is on or off the peg, since it's your butt on the seat that transfers all of your weight to the bike. I like to leave my inside foot off. I'm not sure if it's a technique; it's more like a habit."

3 "When you hit the face of the jump, have your weight in the middle of the bike," Craig said. "Stay neutral, but get ready to pull back a little bit to get the front end high. When the jump is shorter than the bike, you have to pull back and rev it up a little more than normal, or else you'll get kicked forward. If you don't rev it up, the bike might bog, and then for sure you'll be over the bar! You should always squeeze the bike with your knees to keep control of it. This will also help reduce the chances of your bike swapping."

4 "When the shock rebounds, it will kick the bike's back end up higher than normal," Craig continued. "This is the whole object of a seat-bounce jump—to get as much height out of a jump as possible. That's why it's so important to get the front end high on a small jump—so the back end doesn't pass it up."

5 "I usually put my foot back up on the footpeg when I feel the bike has reached the highest point and is headed back down," Craig said. "At this point, I will apply some pressure to the pegs and lean forward to help the bike's front end come back down."

6 "Lean forward and set your sights on where you're gonna land," Craig said. "You want to be fully able to maneuver your bike in the air before you try a jump like this. There's no hitting the rear brake when you seat-bounce. You need to be able to nose the bike with body English. Seat-bouncing is a very advanced technique, and you shouldn't try it unless you're completely comfortable with your bike and know exactly what your suspension is gonna do. I see a lot of amateurs trying to seat-bounce stuff before they're ready with bad results. Be careful.

PHOTOS: DIRT RIDER ARCHIVES

LARRY WARD ON SKIPPING ACROSS OBSTACLES

Often, small doubles or a series of small jumps are difficult to clear entirely. In order to maintain momentum or get a good enough drive to clear the next jump, you have to be able to skip across obstacles without losing your drive. These types of sections are more abundant in supercross, but the technique can be applied to other situations as well. Here, Team Suzuki's Larry Ward shows us the textbook procedure for skipping across jumps.

1 In this section, there are three small jumps before a large triple. The three jumps follow a hairpin turn and the first has a small face. Because of this, it's not possible to triple the section, and if you double the first two jumps and single the third, there is not enough room to get the drive you need to clear the triple. Here, Ward maintains a neutral body position and loads the rear suspension by sitting down when he leaves the face of the first jump. The second jump is larger than the first, so getting enough lift on the first jump is crucial.

2 Ward stands and moves his weight slightly forward after he leaves the first jump. This way he can get the front wheel up and when the rear wheel makes contact with the second jump, the bike will absorb the jump and bring the front end down. The idea is to clear the jump with the entire bike except for the rear wheel. As you can see, Ward barely makes contact with the second jump. He is also under power when the rear wheel makes contact with the second jump. This helps him maintain forward momentum and enables him to clear the third jump. Keeping the power on also keeps the rear wheel loaded, which keeps the bike from kicking when the rear wheel hits the second jump.

3 Ward successfully skips the second jump and prepares to make the landing. After the rear wheel skips off the second jump, Ward starts to shift his weight back to compensate for the force of the wheel hitting the second jump. This also helps level out the bike. As soon as the rear wheel is on the ground, Ward is on the gas hard enough to make the triple 15 feet ahead. This technique can be used to clear small sections of whoops in both motocross and off-road racing. Don't expect to skip jumps to make 70-foot triples on the first day. Start with two small jumps in a row and work your way up.

pro riding secrets
PRS

SOAKING UP SMALL JUMPS WITH TALLON VOHLAND

A jump is a jump, but there are times when altitude is not an ally. In this case, we have a small jump out of a turn before a large tabletop. If the rider simply launches off the first jump, he or she would not land with enough runway to make the flight over the tabletop. On the other hand, just rolling over the first jump does not give the rider the momentum to make the drive to jump. The alternative is to go fast, soak up as much of the jump as possible and make the tabletop. Simple, right? Pay attention as Team FMF/Honda rider Tallon Vohland shows us how it's done.

1 "I don't use this move on all tracks, although it is very handy when situations call for it. I set up for the jump by driving out of the corner hard and quickly get on the pegs. About six feet from the jump I start to wheelie into the jump. At this point my body is in the center of the bike and I have used the clutch and throttle to control my drive into the jump. The key is to keep the front end just high enough that the first contact with the jump will be with the rear wheel."

2 "As my rear wheel approaches the base of the jump, I have moved my weight over the handlebar. Because I am forward on the bike, this helps carry more weight over the jump and allows my legs to soak up most of the impact. Maintaining steady power at this point will carry the front wheel over the jump and keep the bike driving forward. A split second after this shot I will slam the bike into the face of the jump: my skid plate will make contact with the jump. This will help keep the bike driving through the jump as opposed to launching off it."

3 "When the bike starts to crest the top of the jump, I transfer my weight back while using my legs to soak up the upward force of the bike. As you can see from my roost I am still driving forward. I might catch some air off the jump, but it's a lot less than if I'd hit it normally. This technique gets the bike back on the ground with ample room to clear the jump. Never use the brakes or chop the throttle when approaching the jump. If you chop the throttle or use the brakes on the face of the jump, the rear shock may unweight and kick you over the bar. It's best to try the technique going into the jump slow then practice until you find a comfortable speed."

PHOTOS: SCOTT HOFFMAN

pro riding secrets

THE APPROACH

Almost every jump on a motocross track has a turn before it. The amount of real estate before the face of the jump determines how a rider will attack the obstacle. Jumps with a short run and a fair distance to the landing area are the most difficult. In these cases a rider must take full advantage of engine performance, suspension and his or her own strength. A rider may have to use a lot of clutch and/or shift right before the face of the jump. Often a rider must sit down on the face of the jump to compress the suspension for maximum lift. Jumps with longer approaches are much easier because a rider has ample room to accelerate before the jump face. In many situations a rider will brake or let off the power before the jump to avoid overjumping. If a rider has to scrub off speed, it is a good idea to do it prior to the face of the jump, then get back on the gas slightly to enable the bike to leap level and without kicking.

PHOTOS: SCOTT HOFFMAN

54

Understanding how the pros make jumping look so easy is often perplexing to the average rider. A rider's body position, throttle control and weight shift so rapidly when jumping that it is hard to learn merely by watching. We captured 125cc Western Region Supercross Champion Nathan Ramsey frame by frame to illustrate the perfect execution of jumping and landing. But knowing we can't all ride like Ramsey, we added our own commentary to help you take on jumps and landings.

AIRBORNE
The transition of the jump, the angle of the face and the height of the jump are what a rider evaluates to determine the proper approach. Jumps with long transitions and moderate face angles are the easiest. These jumps allow the suspension to settle into the stroke and give the rider time to position his or her body. Stadium-style supercross jumps are harder because the face of the jump is steep and the transition is very rapid. For these jumps, rider strength and body position are critical. The force of the bike hitting the jump compresses or bottoms the suspension, pushing a rider down and back on the bike. Pro riders combat this force by quickly moving their body weight over the handlebar when the bike compresses into the face of the jump. Small, steep jumps give riders trouble with the bike's rear end kicking. This happens when the rider chops or lets off the power too much, releasing the shock on the face of the jump and getting kicked by the rebound. The key is to use a quick burst of power as the rear wheel compresses into the jump face until the bike starts to leave the ground.

MIDAIR CRUISE OR MIDAIR PANIC?
If a rider has hit the jump face correctly, bike and rider will make a perfect arc toward the jump landing. A rider will usually shift his or her weight back slightly and find a neutral position on the bike to set up for the landing. If the execution was done incorrectly, some emergency midair corrections may be necessary. If the bike is front end high, a shift of the body forward or a tap on the rear brake should help correct the problem. If the bike has kicked the rider and the front wheel is too low, a shift back in weight and a slight pull on the bar should help. If the problem is too severe, the panic rev is often necessary. When you hit the gas hard in the air, it creates a torque effect from the engine and the force of the rear wheel spinning. This can bring the rear wheel down and lift the front. These are all techniques that should be practiced on easy jumps.

TOUCHDOWN
At this point a rider knows where he or she is going to land. There are three options here: landing short, perfect or long. If a rider is going to come up short or long, it is a good idea to land rear wheel first. This provides more time to soak up the landing with the body as well as with the suspension. Coming up really short on a double is another place where the panic rev is necessary. Creating a load on the rear wheel stiffens the suspension action and slows down the shock's rebound. This can keep a rider from being kicked off the bike. If a rider lands long, some of the same principles apply. Land with the power on and let the suspension and your legs soak up as much of the impact as possible. Never land stiff, always stay loose. The perfect landing is a no-brainer. The rider already has the bike in position and, depending on whether there's a turn after the jump, lands on or off the gas.

pro riding secrets

AIRING OUT OFF-ROAD

O ff-road races in the west have a variety of road, washout and ditch crossings that need to be negotiated safely. The safety requirements leave two basic choices: Scrub off lots of speed and lose time crossing slowly, or use the speed you have to fly across the hazard.

For some reason (probably to control flash-flood runoff), a channel had been cut across the desert near a Vegas-to-Reno road crossing. When a grader or bulldozer scrapes a road or a ditch in soft, sandy soil, it leaves a raised berm on both sides of the blade path. During the Best in the Desert Vegas-to-Reno course, riders had to negotiate this man-made ditch with a low, soft berm on both sides. The ditch was a short distance from a road crossing, but there was plenty of time to build speed on the approach. Watch as motocrosser-turned-off-road-racer Ty Davis launches over the dip with style.

As he leaves the road crossing, Davis is seated while on the smooth course and accelerating hard. In a race as long as V to R, a rider should sit and rest whenever the terrain allows. As he approaches the hump, Davis stands on the pegs for better control and extended vision. This is the time to decide whether to slow or go.

Davis judges the speed needed and decides to jump the entire obstacle rather than braking for it or pulling a wheelie across it. Once he makes the decision to jump the ditch, he switches from an upright off-road riding stance (that allows maximum vision into the distance and full leg travel for surprise bumps) to a more crouched motocross-style stance. He is balanced in the center of the machine. He uses his legs to load the YZ430 into the face of the berm to allow for more lift. At the speed Davis is traveling, he wants to make sure both wheels clear the far side of the dip.

As the suspension starts to rebound from the impact with the face, Davis gets light on the pegs to help the bike get extra lift. Look closely and you can see that his right boot isn't even touching the footpeg. He can tell immediately that there is plenty of lift to clear the obstacle, so he gets back in the attack stance.

As soon as the bike is back on the ground, Davis is hard on the gas and looking down the trail for the next potential hazard. Note that he hasn't even landed the bike yet, but he is already in a stance ready for the anticipated acceleration. He saved time and energy by choosing to sail across the ditch.

[FACT] Yamaha-mounted Tom Webb won the Desert MC D-37 enduro in 1978.

PHOTOS: KAREL KRAMER

DROP-OFFS

Ever wondered how the pros go so fast? Half of the battle is technique. Tricky sections of a track, such as drop-offs, can highlight a rider's technique. It is *not* always all about speed—the faster you go, the better your chances of winning, right? Wrong. In some situations it is faster to go a little slower than faster. Here Kevin Windham demonstrates the proper style for attacking drop-offs.

PHOTOS: SCOTT HOFFMAN

Windham is a finesse rider who doesn't bulldog the bike around the track. Drop-offs need to be finessed unless you like pounding your body into the ground lap after lap. There are three methods to taking on this type of obstacle. The first is to just slow and roll the crest of the hill and power down the transition. The problem is that most riders have to scrub too much speed to roll the crest. This technique will not win races.

The second technique is to just blast off the lip and either land on the flat or the lower section of the transition. In some cases, this can be the fastest way to attack the section. However, if the drop-off is too deep, landing on the flat or down in the transition can be very hard on the body and the bike.

The most favorable technique is to leave the face of the jump as fast as possible to land on the down side of the drop-off before the transition to flat.

As you can see from the sequence, K-Dub tilts and floats his bike off the lip of the jump to get the least amount of lift off the jump. Once he is in the air he maintains a neutral body position to allow the bike to stay level in the air. As he gets closer to the ground, Windham extends his body to prepare for the landing. Before the rear tire makes contact with the ground, Windham grabs a handful of throttle to keep the bike driving forward. Before his front wheel touches down you can see the roost blasting from his rear wheel. As the bike makes full contact with the ground, Windham uses his legs as well as the suspension to soak up the impact from the landing. With the bike fully planted on the ground, K-Dub pulls himself back into the attack position and powers off to the next section of the track.

Windham's technique can actually prove to be faster than just blasting off the face and flying to the bottom of the jump. When the first rider is floating through the air, the second rider is getting back on the ground and accelerating forward. Placing the bike back on the ground sooner also helps the rider get the bike settled and in position sooner for the next obstacle. Start off with rolling a drop-off and slowly increase your speed until you have timed the perfect place to land.

57

Hot Tips

CHAPTER FOUR

Jeremy McGrath: Braking tricks .59
ISDE Training camp 60
Powder surfing 62
Guy Cooper riding tip handbook .63
Larry Roeseler and Ty Davis on team tactics and desert racing 69
Paul Edmondson on how to wheelie 70
Cold weather riding tips 71
Dick Burleson on Braking 74
Hot weather riding tips 75
The champs guide to play riding 76
Guy Cooper on line choice 79
Back to basics by Gary Semics .80
Suspension S.O.S. 82
Prepare for muddy days 87
Sand washes with Destry Abbott 88
How to handle whoops 89
Doing the dab 90
Deep rutted tracks 91
Maintain drive with standing drives 92
Night Advice 93
Speed Secrets 95

JEREMY McGRATH
BRAKING TRICKS

The faster you go, the faster you must stop. But simply clamping hard on the binders isn't going to win races. There are a number of subtle tricks the fast guys employ to get them around a track faster.

We caught Honda's Jeremy McGrath during practice for the Orlando supercross, demonstrating a mild brake slide. It's not done to be flashy, like his Nac Nac; rather, it serves a purpose, which in this case is to help set the bike up early for the upcoming corner that has a small rut-berm forming.

Here's a head-on view of McGrath's approach. He's using both brakes in addition to the clutch, and the rear end is obviously stepped out to the side because he's set it up with a slight brake slide. Though it's a bit hard to see, he's standing.

From the side, he closes in on the corner. He's still standing—and will remain so for the next few feet—with his legs, back and elbows slightly bent to better absorb any braking bumps. Notice that he's looking ahead to the corner.

At this point, McGrath begins to ease off the brakes and roll the throttle back on—notice how the fork's starting to extend. In addition, take note that he's kept his head over the handlebar despite keeping most of his weight rearward.

McGrath's dropped into the beginning of the rut-berm now. He's using a combination of slight braking in conjunction with a gradual opening of the throttle the closer he gets to the apex. He's also started to drop into the forward part of the seat.

Fully seated in the front part of the bike for the most precise steering, McGrath eyes the turn's apex. He's still on the throttle and brakes simultaneously, though he'll soon be completely off the brakes and accelerating as hard as possible—even before reaching the apex. He plants his knee hard against the radiator shroud to help force the bike over, and he'll soon scan ahead to the next obstacle.

PHOTOS: KEN FAUGHT

Off-Road Prep Tips
TEAM GREEN SURRENDERS THE WINNING SECRETS

Kawasaki's Team Green technicians have an enviable record of off-road success. The one or two factory-supported bikes that race in (and usually win) the team–type events like SCORE's Baja race or Best in the Desert's Vegas-to-Reno and Tonopah 300 are prepped and modified in-house. We followed along as Craig Martin put the finishing touches on Ty Davis and Paul Krause's winning Vegas-to-Reno mount. These professionally modified machines offer greater reliability and mechanical protection than stock—plus they can change a rear wheel and rider *and* get a full tank of fuel in just a 17-second pit stop! Even though these bikes are prepped for the deserts of the American West, the methods and mods used should make for fast pit stops and sure survival in any sort of off-road competition.

1 Here's the finished, soon-to-be-a-winner Vegas-to-Reno Kawasaki KX500. Well, almost finished. Team Green usually slips sections of high-temperature rubber hose over the pipe springs to reduce their vibration. This time it didn't, though, and the bike finished the race without springs.

2 Team Green adds a chain-guide reinforcing plate on the outside of the guard like most people do, but then welds this additional mount to the inside of the swingarm and fabricates this inner plate, as well. This requires fabrication skill and an experienced heliarc operator.

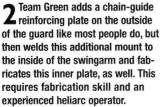

3 Some of the finest work that Team Green lavishes upon this machine allows ultraspeedy rear-wheel changes. The caliper-side chain-adjuster block is drilled and countersunk to allow a Phillips screw to sit flush. The rear-brake caliper mount is lined up perfectly with the chain-adjuster block by slipping the axle through both, then drilling and tapping the caliper mount. The screw is doused in thread-locking compound and lightly tightened. The two parts are kept perfectly aligned but still allow for easy chain adjustment.

6 These trick wheel spacers are available from Terrycable. The rounded edges help the wheel fit in easily, but a lip on the wheel side lets the seal grip more securely. It isn't quite as foolproof as the stock KTM press-fit spacers, but it's the next-best thing.

7 Though the mods to the other side of the swingarm are trick, they can be realized in most riders' garages. The chain side looks a lot simpler but actually requires more tools and know-how. On the sprocket side, an exact replica of the standard chain-adjuster block is machined from steel, then it has an axle nut welded on. The top and bottom edges of the swingarm are drilled and tapped for 5mm bolts. These are tightened just enough to keep the chain block in place for wheel changes but still allow the chain to be adjusted.

8 The mods to the front wheel and axle are few. The end of the axle is welded up and threaded so that all the hardware on this side of the wheel uses the same size T-handle. We suspected that the thin sleeve on the axle was something real trick, but the truth is that all Kawasaki's spare front wheels used the old–style small-axle wheel bearings. The sleeve simply allows the old axle to be used in the new fork. Each of the pits is stocked with sleeves and axles in case a rider with a stock bike needs to exchange a wheel.

4 Note that the rear side of the caliper mounting bracket and the trailing edge of the brake pads are beveled to allow the wheel and spacers to slide in easily. Also, check out the axle end peeking out of the mounting bracket. A pointed nylon "bullet," machined and fitted into the end of the hollow axle, lets the axle slide in even if all the parts are not perfectly aligned. The axle just centers the parts as it goes through.

5 A top view of the entire brake-side quick-change reveals the axle spacer with a rounded edge, the beveled caliper mount and the large nut welded onto the end of the axle. The nut isn't a necessity, but it allows the Team Green pits to use the same tools to change these axles and remove the axle nuts as they do on standard KXs. There is also some brake trickery here. The hex-head stainless steel brake pins are pretty standard aftermarket stuff these days from Moose Racing, Motion Pro and Terrycable, but check out the little safety-wire wrap on the outboard brake pad. The pad that rests against the caliper's piston has a thin sheet of ceramic insulation between the pad's back and the stainless steel anti-squeal plate. Whenever Team Green changes pads, it removes the insulator from the old pad and runs a double insulator on the new pad. That protects the caliper and brake fluid from extreme heat. The anti-squeal plate doesn't fit as it should with both insulators installed, so it is safety-wired. Great idea for Baja or woods competition.

9 Many motocross teams employ the welded-glide-plate trick. This piece of very thin steel serves three purposes: It protects the cases, provides the same ground clearance as stock and strengthens the frame. The KDX–style crash bars for the coolant pump and the ignition cover are fabricated in-house and welded to the frame.

10 The radiators are the site of much careful detailing. All the mounting brackets are reinforced, and a billet-aluminum item replaces the plastic plug in the top of the left one. Not only are the shrouds carefully spaced to keep the large fuel tank from pressing against them, but the tops of the radiator louvers are trimmed away, as well. Vibration and wind pressure can cause the louvers to rub holes into the aluminum radiator. (Note that the louver is safety wired.)

11 The silencer's attachment gets a lot of attention. You can see the small gusset welded to the end cap to help strengthen the pipe-to-

silencer mount, but you can't really see that the silencer core is actually brazed along the entire seam; the stocker is only spot-welded. The team bikes get new packing for each event, too. Similar mods would be wise for ISDE competition.

12 The completed silencer is mounted with this billet bracket from Terrycable to prevent breakage. If a spark arrestor is required, it can be welded to the end of the silencer can. Why take a chance on disqualification for something as dull as losing a spark arrestor?

13 A lot more work went into the footpeg area than meets the eye. You can see the safety wire in the brake pedal/master cylinder junction and the Pro Circuit billet-steel footpegs, but a factory–style billet-steel footpeg mount hides from view. Terrycable sells this replica of the factory motocross units, but the frame must be ground completely smooth before installation. Only the most professional welding job will suffice, as well.

The aluminum brake pedal has a flat for the brake-pedal-height adjusting bolt to rest on. On this bike the back of the flat is heliarced thicker, then draw-filed flat to give the bolt head a solid resting place.

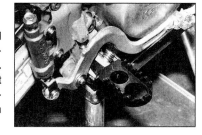

14 We've heard of sealing the air-filter sealing ring to the airboot before, but we've never seen the entire gap between the airbox and the sealing ring filled in. It makes great sense, since it makes cleaning the airbox much easier and provides one less place for dirt that could end up in the airboot and get caught.

15 Check out the detailing on this clutch cable. This strengthens the cable and seals out dirt. The extended clutch-actuating arm eases the clutch pull, too. These trick pointed studs holding in the reed cage replace the standard bolts, making lining up the cage easier and top end replacements much quicker.

16 Abrasion-resistant spiral-wrap protects the hose from the rear-brake fluid reservoir to the master cylinder. Stronger automotive worm-drive–type hose clamps replace the stock clamps on both sides of the carb.

17 Shimming the motor mounts and head stays keeps stress off the mounts and tubes. Note that every wire and loose part is zip-tied, including the spark-plug cap.

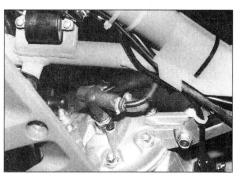

As you might imagine, the KXs sport all the accoutrements expected on nicely prepped race bikes (e.g., hand guards, safety-wired and glued grips, a Scotts steering stabilizer, etc.). Mostly, though, these bikes stand out for attention to detail and well-designed modifications. No wonder Team Green is on top!

Obviously, some of these mods are only applicable to long, high-speed events, but most (like the quick-change wheels) would help any off-road rider or racer. They apply especially to multiday races like the ISDE. Now get out there in the garage and make that bike trick!

POWDER SURFING

Glen Helen Raceway Park features a large, banked, bowl turn that provides some spectacular action with the right riders between the banners. While most amateur riders opt for the low, more hard-packed line, faster riders like Team Kawasaki's Damon Huffman, go for the high road and rail the loose, powdery silt that gets pushed to the top. Going high expends less energy, takes less time and, as Huffman reports, "If you go down low on the hard-packed stuff, you risk fighting with the bike. It's easy to get the bike into a slide because the corner is flat and slippery. Going up in the powder keeps your wheels in line, and, besides, it's more fun!"

1 Huffman carries more speed into the corner when using the higher line: "I let off the throttle just a little entering the turn, but I don't even bother with the brakes," Huffman says. "You can carry way more speed into the corner if you go high. It is important to look ahead.

2 "I stay standing up pretty far into the corner," Huffman notes. "You should be in a gear that will pull you steadily. Don't rev the bike too hard; it's better to be at about half throttle. I sit down at the apex of the corner, but I stay more centered than normal because riding up front will cause the front end to tuck.

3 "Be prepared, just in case the berm gets extra deep. Here, the bike started to dig deeper into the powder, so I compensated with a little more throttle and a slip of the clutch. Keep your leg out, just in case the bike gets squirrelly.

4 "If you go high, you'll exit the corner much faster. This is where looking ahead really pays off. In this corner, there's a tabletop jump right afterwards, so I stand up as soon as possible to prepare for the jump. Hitting it from the outside is trickier, since you're going faster, so it's important to be standing up and ready for the face."

PHOTOS: DIRT RIDER ARCHIVES

GUY COOPER RIDING TIP HANDBOOK

Most dirt riders would like to be Guy Cooper for a week. After all, the Suzuki racer has plenty of toys and the land (thus, the tracks) on which to abuse them daily. He has motocross, supercross, enduro, trials and even dirt track courses/ sections that get pounded regularly by him and anyone who happens to be visiting.

Besides being the consummate motorcycle enthusiast, "Coop" is also a member of an elite squad: He's one of the few who've won National championships in both motocross and off-road racing (he topped the AMA 125cc National MX Series in 1990 and won this year's AMA National Reliability Enduro Series 125cc crown). That, in our books, spells versatility.

A visit to Cooperland in Oklahoma proves beyond any doubt that he has the ideal training facility. Being the host that he is, Cooper was more than willing to demonstrate and share some of the techniques he's used to win two National championships and hundreds of individual races throughout his career. We think you'll find them both entertaining and informative.

PHOTO: MARK KARIYA

1

RESTARTING AFTER A STALL

It's happened to all of us—and it'll happen again: You're cruising up a nasty trail, a rock or ditch jumps out in front of you, and you stall your engine. Great. What do you do? Getting going again can be tricky, with lots of wheelspin and no forward motion. But Suzuki's Guy Cooper demonstrates a better, more efficient method here.

1 "I came up to this off-camber uphill and stalled, which is typical if you don't have a lot of speed," Cooper begins. "In this situation I didn't know what was [beyond the top]. I'm already off to the high side of the hill. I could start the bike right here, but I don't want to because when you start the bike in this position, it's difficult…and the second you pull in the clutch to start it, you're going to roll backward."

2 "I push the bike back to a flat spot, which is only a few feet back. (This photo shows that I'm using the rock and my foot to push back down the hill.)"

3 Cooper reaches a flatter spot on the trail, though it's still off-camber, which is hard to see in the photo (it does drop away on his right). "My hand on the tree enables the bike to sit almost straight up and down; it's easy to start it, and by [rolling back to] here I can clutch it and get that little bit of a drive to get over this rock ledge."

2

3

PHOTOS: DIRT RIDER ARCHIVES

WHEELYING INTO—AND OVER—SMALL BOULDERS

If a small boulder suddenly appears in the trail, most riders will go around it. This might be the perfect opportunity to pass a guy—or close in on him, at least.

The problem, of course, is making it over the boulder cleanly the first time. This is when Cooper's trials experience pays off.

1 "The way I learned to do this was on my trials bike," he states. "We're going to call this rock two feet high (it's somewhere around there). If this rock is two feet high, then a little more than two feet back, I need to start pulling a wheelie into it. So, it's at about a 45-degree angle that you want to set [the bike] into this rock. You don't want to [carry] the front wheel all the way over the top, because if you do, of course, the next thing that's going to hit is the middle of the frame. So what [I'm] going to do is use the front wheel to help elevate the motorcycle. When the front wheel hits the edge of the rock, it's going to compress the fork. The rear wheel is on the ground. You can see that when I started to pull the wheelie that close to the rock it loaded the rear suspension. This is a little bit tall on the rock. A trials rider will put about eight inches of tire tread at the top of this rock [on the face]. What that'll do is really load the front suspension. It'll absorb [the hit], and, since you're at a 45-degree angle, the [rebounding] motion will be upward."

2 "As the front tire rolls over the top of the rock, the rebounding of the fork and the rear suspension tosses the motorcycle at least a foot into the air. The rear wheel is now completely off the ground [in this photo]; there was nothing there [on the ground] to lift the bike off the ground. It was just the fact that everything was loaded, and when the front wheel pulled up, the whole motorcycle came off the ground. With the momentum that's pulling forward as the front wheel goes down, the rear wheel grabs. Right when the rear wheel hits [the rock], the throttle is on about a quarter… and my finger is on the clutch (to keep the engine from either stalling or revving too high). If I held [the throttle] wide open when [the rear wheel] hit here, it would just start spinning, and I'd get no traction.

HEADS UP!

Those who only care about diddling in the daisies and absorbing the beautiful scenery can skip this one. This tip's for those riders interested in reducing the amount of time required to negotiate any given section of trail. Though it's a simple thing, it's something that most of us must constantly remind ourselves of: The faster you want to go, the farther ahead you must look.

1 "My head's up," Cooper points out, "so I'm at speed here. The rock that I'm hitting here I already saw 20 or 30 feet back; I knew I could hit it at speed. Once you're on the rock, you shouldn't be looking at [it anymore]. So the next thing I need to look at is the trail way down the road."

2 Even in the previous frame, Cooper could see the group of ugly rocks in the lower middle portion of this photo. They're not something even he wants to hit, and there's a nice path beside them. "As I get closer, I get on the brakes and slow way down because you can't see the back side [of the boulder the rocks are sitting on]. At speed, from way back, it looked good."

3 Here, Cooper can finally see that there's nothing to worry about so he gets back on it, wheelying off the boulder. "The whole point you have to remember is, your eyes have to be looking way down the road because the trail speed for the last mile could've been second and third gear. This is a first-gear/slow-down/drop-off-the-edge-and-continue situation. Pay attention to what's in *front* of you. If there's nothing to be worried about in front of you, the speed can be higher. You have to make note of what's way down the trail."

LEAPING INTO THE GREAT UNKNOWN

Drop-offs are generally no problem: You simply gas it before taking off and land on the rear wheel, just like a simple jump.

The problem comes when the intended landing area is completely grown over with bushes and vines, or when it contains a small boulder field. Leaping into the great unknown is a dicey proposition that can lead to broken cases, smashed frame tubes or severe bodily harm.

In the example pictured here at Cooperland, Guy watches as Dick Burleson takes a flying leap. Follow along as "Coop" describes the situation.

1 "This is a rock face. It's level ground on top; it's the edge of a hill coming down…and there's another eight or 10 feet of runout at the bottom.

"The problem when you get into this type of stuff is that it's leaf-covered vines and stuff with boulders at the bottom. You really have to be careful and *see* what you're jumping into. This requires very low speed when dropping off this rock. We eyed up this drop-off before we did it the first time. We got off the bikes and looked at what we would be dropping off of, then looked to see where the rocks were and plan how we would slide through the bottom."

2 "You [have] to carry the front end high enough that you [don't] endo off the ledge. There's no way you could ride off it. It doesn't show in the leaves, but…some of this ivy and stuff [at the bottom] is 12 or 18 inches [thick]. So the key is to carry the front end high, like what you'd do with a slow wheelie. You want to make sure you're in first gear, that you have a finger on the clutch and the throttle on to where it'll for sure pull you all the way across the rock. It can't just be a dart wheelie (where you gas it and jump off) because you can't carry a lot of speed off it. So we're barely pulling a wheelie off the rock, but the motor is pulling to hold that front end up as we go over it."

3 "Here it looks like [the front end has] dropped. That's because right when the rear wheel goes over the ledge, you just chop the throttle and let the front end go. You have to make sure the front wheel is far enough out so that when you do start to drop it, you're not in a full endo mode. The opposite could apply if you continued to rev and carried that front end at a high rate of speed off the rock—you're gonna jump too far down the hill, and there're…obstacles down there. So you have to know the length of the bike and plan how to get the front end back onto the ground. Once the front end's on the ground, you can steer the bike around the obstacles. You have to make sure your weight's back—you're expecting the bike to land on the front wheel—but once the front end touches, you can get on the brakes and steer out of the obstacles."

SEATED AND STANDING JUMPS

Cooper is best known as a leaper, and it's certainly something he enjoys practicing. He demonstrated two different ways to attack one jump on one of his tracks, since most obstacles can be tackled in more than one way.

"I don't like to be the teacher on jumps [if students] try it on every jump [afterward]," he emphasizes. "A sitdown jump is for the advanced rider only, and it's also for specific jumps. You don't try to hit triples sitting down.

"Sitting down on the bike will load the suspension differently; it will compress differently, and the bike will leave the jump a lot differently. It's something that's good to try on uphill doubles or low-speed stuff where you need to compress the suspension.

"Take a three-foot-high jump, [for example, where] you stand up coming into it. The [suspension] compresses. Your legs and arms are your personal suspension, in theory, and they absorb a lot of the impact going into the jump, so that your trajectory leaving the jump will not be enhanced.

"You hit that same jump—same speed—sitting down, and all the force is immediately transmitted into the motorcycle. So the suspension goes down farther, it loads the motorcycle more, and...as you leave the jump, the suspension [rebounds]. It's the same as hitting a four-foot jump because when you compress into it, it now rebounds [more] as you take off."

1 "You can tell in the picture here that my suspension is nearly completely bottomed. It's just a simple tabletop here, but I'm really loading the suspension going into it. The throttle must be wide open because, when you compress like this, the motorcycle wants to slow down—more so than if you were standing up. In a sitdown jump, nine times out of 10 you want to jump as far as you can, and you use the sitdown technique to get the added height."

2 "When I start to leave the jump, the suspension rebounds immediately. It pulls right back up and takes my body weight up with it (notice that Cooper is well off the seat here). You and the motorcycle get a lifted effect whenever you sit down to load the motorcycle [when hitting a jump]. I expected the motorcycle to rebound like it did, so it's not unusual to see the front end this high for me. Also, we're not going that fast—I'm in second gear here. Everything's being lifted more upward than it is being propelled forward."

3 "I rolled my shoulders [forward] here to bring my body weight forward; it drops the front wheel. Whenever you're in the air [you want to make] sure the throttle is off to level the motorcycle out."

4 "You can see here that a little smoke comes back on. It's because when I land on the downside off the jump, with the front end down, I can accelerate down the back side. That's an important part of landing front wheel first or what's called 'downsiding the jump.' If you can downside with the front end down under acceleration, you won't loop out. If I jumped level and had the throttle on, well, I'd be sitting on my butt."

5 Though this photo wasn't taken at the same instant as the first photo, it's apparent that standing while hitting the jump doesn't compress the suspension nearly as much. Keep in mind, though, that the sitdown technique is an advanced one to be employed only in certain situations.

PHOTOS: DIRT RIDER ARCHIVES

LARRY ROESELER AND TY DAVIS AND ON TEAM TACTICS AND DESERT RACING

Don't ride in dust, if possible. Use any breeze to your advantage, as it'll carry dust away. That helps both your vision and air filter life. Watch the helmet of the rider ahead of you for sudden dips or jumps that may be ahead.

Team Green and Pro Circuit provided a brief seminar on tactics and setup tips for desert/team racing the night before the Team Green/Danny Hamel Memorial Tonopah 300. Ty Davis and Larry Roeseler shared their overall insights, while Pro Circuit's Jim "Bones" Bacon delved into solving suspension queries.

While these tips are geared toward the desert racer, many of them are general in nature and can apply to the motocrosser or woods fanatic, as well.

"BONES" ON SUSPENSION

Since Kawasakis in particular have a heat-compensating device in their shocks, Bacon recommends setting the sag on KXs before they're ridden, when the shock is cold. Otherwise, you're liable to be off five millimeters.

Make sure the bike's level before you set sag, of course, and have the rider (in full gear) sit forward on the seat with his hands on the grips, balancing the bike himself so his feet are barely brushing the ground. An assistant will have to take the before and after measurements to determine sag. Bacon likes to run KX500s with a little less sag than normally recommended for a bit more effective range of travel.

When Ty talks, people listen—even vets like Larry Roeseler. Actually, Davis and Roeseler helped conduct a prerace desert-racing clinic at Tonopah.

PHOTOS: MARK KARIYA

When setting up the suspension, you've got to "look at the course," if at all possible. For a team race, realize that "suspension will be a compromise" and lean toward setting the bike up for the heavier rider.

You can help keep the bike up in the travel by using rebound damping that's relatively light and quick. "Compression is something you'll have to play with," Bacon notes. "Compression changes are the easiest and quickest to do during a race."

Don't be afraid to pop the fork's dust seals off to clean underneath them, especially after a muddy race. Keeping track of things will make it easy to know when things should be replaced as a preventative measure. Bacon, for instance, recommends a shock service after 10 hours of hard riding.

DAVIS AND ROESELER ON RIDING

Larry Roeseler is on the semi-retired list of motorcycle racers, but he's still faster than most. Besides natural ability and plenty of practice riding, he's a proponent of judicious training, too. "It's really important not to overtrain," he insists. "It's important to have good rest, as well."

Hydration is vital to lasting the duration of a long, hot 100-miler, or however long the race is. "Drink lots of fluids the day before a race," LR recommends. He likes sports drinks but realizes that everybody's different: "Experiment to find what you like and what works for you."

As for riding itself, "My riding tip for the weekend is: Use a Scotts steering damper." What dampers do is reduce a bike's tendency to headshake and deflect off hidden rocks; thus, they reduce the fatigue factor.

Roeseler also suggests using PC Racing Filterskins (dry) on air filters for dusty races. Also, "I highly recommend bleeding your brakes after every race."

When it comes to reading terrain, Roeseler says, "You've got to eliminate the element of surprise. Part of it is good eyesight, good vision. I tend to look up and down pretty regularly."

Scanning the terrain ahead is critical. The faster you go, the farther ahead you must look.

Realizing that not everyone can be in front in clean air, Davis says to watch the helmet of the rider in front of you. When it's dusty, his helmet is often the only thing you'll be able to see, and you'll be able to tell with a fair degree of certainty what the terrain is like by studying that helmet. Whether you stay on his back wheel or just out of his dust cloud depends on you.

Of course, goggle prep is vitally important in dust. "Roll Off's (sic) are a big no-no here," Davis insists. "Dust will always get in between the [Roll Off's] film and the lens," which means it'll scratch the lens when you advance the film and you'll be trying to peer through two dust-covered surfaces, one of them scratched.

Instead, Davis says, "Put Moose Racing's new Dust'r, Armor All, Static Guard or something like that on the lens and do it a couple of times. You won't believe how well it works. You just have to reach up and wipe off the lens with your sleeve, and it's clear."

To help prevent dust from contaminating the inside of the goggle, Davis uses a *light* coating of Vaseline on the vent foam. If it's going to be a high-speed race, he'll apply silicone sealant to the top vent foam.

1 Before Edmondson starts his wheelie, he positions himself in the middle of the bike and gets comfortable. Because a wheelie takes so much balance, you must make sure that you're comfortable before you start. He starts his wheelie in second gear, riding at a slow pace. To begin, he pulls in his clutch lever, twists the throttle to build revs and pulls back on the handlebar at the same time that he releases the clutch lever. Though these photos were shot on flat ground, it's easier to learn on a slight uphill grade.

PAUL EDMONDSON ON HOW TO WHEELIE

In most of our "Pro Riding Secrets" articles, we present riding techniques for race conditions. Play riding, though, is a great way for riders to learn their personal limits while gaining a better feel for their machines, as well. We guarantee that every top rider devotes a certain amount of time each week to play riding. Heck, some pros play as much as three days a week! Team Suzuki's newest recruit, World Enduro Champion Paul Edmondson, spends a great deal of time doing what he loves best: wheelying.

Riding a wheelie is the first thing we all tried to do on a motorcycle, but most of us still can't ride a slow, controlled wheelie. Wheelying teaches riders how to master the controls in a hurry, as well as acquainting them with the principle of balance. Balance is the key to controlling your motorcycle, and besides—riding a wheelie is just plain fun. Here, Edmondson shows us the right way to ride a wheelie.

2 As the front wheel begins to come up, you need to slide back on the seat to gain better leverage. The most important thing about riding a wheelie is keeping your foot on the rear-brake pedal. When you pull back on the bar, you must also keep good control of the throttle. Use the rear brake and throttle to keep the wheelie in control.

3 While you're in the wheelie, you must constantly work the throttle, clutch and rear brake to keep things going. Try to find your balance point and then maintain it: This is critical. If you start to drop the front end, tug on the bar again and apply throttle to get it back up. To come out of a wheelie, simply chop the throttle or hit the rear-brake pedal hard and the front end will return to the ground.

BUNDLE UP!

One of the most challenging things about the *Dirt Rider* 24-hour shootout is the nasty temperatures test riders encounter during the nighttime hours. Once the sun sets, riders not only have to worry about the decreased visibility, but uncomfortably cold temperatures, as well. Luckily, the storms that hammered California in the days prior to the event let up, and testers didn't have to contend with rain, too. Still, the *DR* staff prepared for the nastiest of riding conditions. The following are a few of our favorite cold-weather setups.

EYE PROTECTION

Goggles: Traditionalists will insist on wearing goggles at all times. Several little tricks can make standard "gogs" more effective in cold weather. Naturally, treating the lens with a no-fog cloth helps, but even the best-treated lens might still steam up. "I really like Smith Violators," *DR*'s Editorial Director Tom Webb says. "The Violator frame allows you to either remove the foam or install more porous foam without ruining the frame permanently." Scott, Smith and Oakley all produce quite effective double-paned and vented lenses, but all tend to scratch easier than standard units do. Also, hard work will sweat out the inside, leaving perspiration drops and sheeting to contend with. In misty or rainy situations, Smith Roll-Off's (sic) equipped with a Roll-Off's visor are unbeatable. The next best thing? A lens that has been well treated with Rain-X. Tear offs are a no-no while rain-riding off-road, but for moto, Scott Quick Load tear offs keep the muck from sneaking in between the multiple layers, and Oakley has a new tear-off visor that works just like a Roll-Off's visor.

Moose Eye Shields are available in clear, yellow and persimmon, and are DOT approved for on- and off-road use.

Oakley glasses come in endless frame and lens combinations, many of which are ideal for off-road motorcycle use. Oakley's optics yield excellent vision.

MSR's Pak-Jak is a staple among the *Dirt Rider* testing staff. This is the Gore-Tex version, but a water-resistant model is also available. The Pak-Jak works in a wide range of temperatures.

The Moose Racing Fleece vest is another favorite. Its front panel features a nylon shell that blocks wind and resists water.

AXO Sport's Padlock All Weather glove boasts an extra-long neoprene wrist cuff and a nonvented design. Toasty!

Some regular off-road gloves work well in cold conditions. Models, like the MSR System 6 glove, that feature extensive padding and paneling on the back of the hand do a good job of blocking the wind.

Wearing full-length Lycra bicycle tights can both keep you warm and eliminate the need for knee-brace socks for CTi wearers. Moose Fleece socks are a Godsend when the temperatures begin to dip.

Moose Racing's Gore-Tex pants are the best on the market, period. Thanks to the generous amounts of waterproof-tape–lined spandex, the pants offer little resistance to movement. The Moose pants fit over knee braces, no problem.

71

Riding Glasses: Dick Burleson and Tom Webb are both strong believers in riding glasses. Though Burleson has ditched his infamous prescription peepers in favor of contact lenses, "The King" still opts for a set of Moose Eye Shields in really foul conditions. When do glasses beat out goggles? "When it's really, really cold out, or even raining, I'll whip out a pair of Oakleys," Webb says. "Glasses allow a lot more air to flow through, so they hardly ever fog up, even in sections where you're really working hard. They're also easy to clean, as they lack the foam that attracts major buildup. All they need is a quick swipe with a no-fog cloth to rid them of moisture." Both Moose and Oakley glasses are shatterproof and on- and off-road legal (having passed DOT impact tests). While clear is the most popular color, yellow and persimmon lens tints are available for low-light conditions.

PIGS IN A BLANKET

Ever stand barefoot on a tile kitchen floor? If you have, you know that your body heat can be sucked out of your feet faster than Mental can down two Double Doubles, fries and a 55-gallon drum of Coke. The *DR* staff's *absolute* favorite way to keep their little piggies warm is Moose's Fleece riding socks. Though they don't stretch and special care must be taken in order to find the correct size, the Moose socks are a Godsend when the temperatures begin to drop. Numb toes are a thing of the past, and it doesn't matter if your feet are wet or dry when you put the socks on. The fleece uses body heat to warm the air between its layers, even if your feet are stone cold! Also, if you're lucky, you might be able to find an ancient pair of Hallman Feet Heet neoprene riding booties at an overstocked dealership. Though THOR (formerly Hallman) doesn't sell the booties anymore, they're still around here and there. Unlike fleece socks, however, the Feet Heet don't disperse perspiration.

TOASTY HANDS

Other important extremities to keep warm are your hands—after all, that's what's keeping you on your bike, right? Any good glove with lots of plastic on the fingers and top of the hand works better than units with lots of webbing and a lack of plastic. A couple of cold-weather–specific gloves do command attention out there, however. AXO Sport's Padlock All Weather glove is a heavy-duty version of its popular MX glove, but the All Weather doesn't feature the MX's

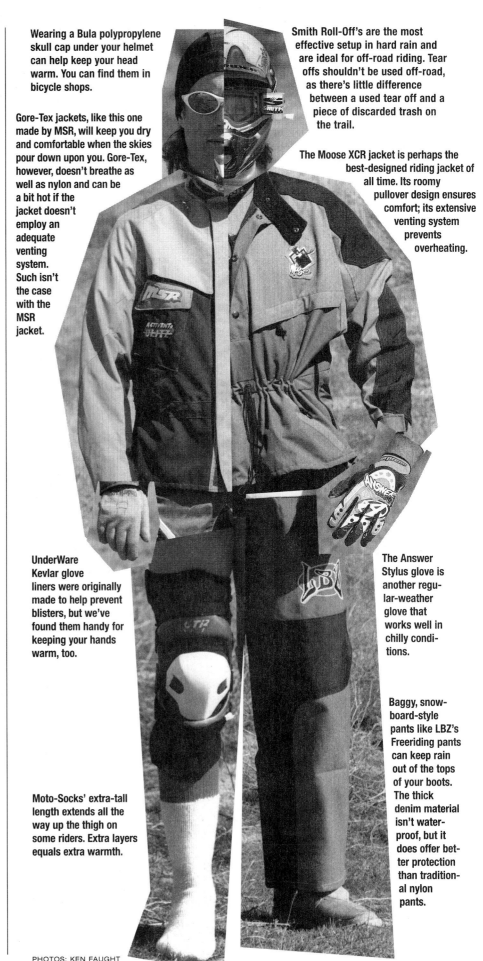

Wearing a Bula polypropylene skull cap under your helmet can help keep your head warm. You can find them in bicycle shops.

Gore-Tex jackets, like this one made by MSR, will keep you dry and comfortable when the skies pour down upon you. Gore-Tex, however, doesn't breathe as well as nylon and can be a bit hot if the jacket doesn't employ an adequate venting system. Such isn't the case with the MSR jacket.

UnderWare Kevlar glove liners were originally made to help prevent blisters, but we've found them handy for keeping your hands warm, too.

Moto-Socks' extra-tall length extends all the way up the thigh on some riders. Extra layers equals extra warmth.

Smith Roll-Off's are the most effective setup in hard rain and are ideal for off-road riding. Tear offs shouldn't be used off-road, as there's little difference between a used tear off and a piece of discarded trash on the trail.

The Moose XCR jacket is perhaps the best-designed riding jacket of all time. Its roomy pullover design ensures comfort; its extensive venting system prevents overheating.

The Answer Stylus glove is another regular-weather glove that works well in chilly conditions.

Baggy, snow-board-style pants like LBZ's Freeriding pants can keep rain out of the tops of your boots. The thick denim material isn't waterproof, but it does offer better protection than traditional nylon pants.

PHOTOS: KEN FAUGHT

extensive venting system. Additionally, its neoprene wrist cuff is nearly two inches longer, helping seal the warmth in and the elements out. Webb and *DR* Test Editor Donn Maeda depend on these gloves when the weather turns nasty. Feature Editor Karel Kramer, meanwhile, prefers good old-fashioned wraparound hand guards. You know, the ones that look like giant elephant ears. "Those things are the best when it comes to keeping the wind off your hands," Kramer says. "They don't look very stylish, but I'll take 'em!" Hot Grips are an even more effective—albeit costly—alternative. When hooked up to your bike's wire harness, Hot Grips keep your hands toasty, even in the rain. They can also dry out wet gloves!

DRESS CODES

Cool Weather: When the temperatures are chilly but there's no rain in the forecast, we have all come to love riding vests. The Moose Fleece vest is completely unrestrictive, can be worn over or under a chest protector and has a water-resistant front panel that does an excellent job of taking the bite out of windchill. Its four huge pockets come in handy for trail riding. An avid mountain biker, Webb will throw on a pair of full-length Lycra tights underneath his regular MX pants, as well.

Cool Weather/Chance of Rain: An MSR Pak-Jak is the perfect complement to the Moose Fleece vest and Lycra tights if rain threatens. Light and unrestrictive, the Pak-Jak will keep you dry without causing overheating. Choose from two versions: water-resistant or fully waterproof Gore-Tex. Both feature a zippered neck opening that can provide extra venting if you overheat. If the skies never let loose, the Pak-Jak can be rolled into its own pocket and carried in a fanny pack. We've used the Pak-Jak when the temps got downright frosty (snow) with great success.

Cold Weather: This is where regular, nonGore-Tex jackets come in. When the temperatures dip too low for the vest/windbreaker combo, we like to throw on a standard riding jacket. The Moose XCR pullover coat is generously cut, fits over chest protectors and features an extensive venting system to prevent overheating. Its plethora of well-designed pockets comes in handy, too. We also like the standard jackets from Sinisalo and AXO Sport. Both feature removable sleeves, making them eligible for vest weather, as well. The Sinisalo jacket of soft Cordura is one of the most comfortable we've tried. The AXO coat, meanwhile, features a subdued black-and-gray color scheme that makes it perfect for dual-sport riders. When the temperatures dip even lower, a combination of jackets and vests can apply.

Cold and Rainy: In steady rain, a good set of Gore-Tex riding gear can't be beat. Plenty of companies produced Gore-Tex riding apparel at one time, but because of its high cost (and subsequent low demand), only Moose and MSR continue to turn out the stuff. Both companies' jackets offer excellent waterproofing and will keep you absolutely dry and toasty—with the exception of unruly droplets that wick under the cuffs in a constant downpour. The Moose pants, however, get the nod from the *DR* staff, as the wide spandex leg panels fit nicely over knee braces. The downfall of Gore-Tex is usually its nonstretch character, but

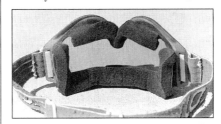

Tom Webb cuts small frame sections out of the bottom of his goggles in order to eliminate fogging in cold temperatures.

Tearing the foam out of the top of your goggles will work wonders for fogging, but will ruin the pair for regular use. Make sure you have extras before you go "tear happy."

Smith's Violator goggle's interchangeable foam system allows you to change the density of the foam inserts. The more porous inserts help prevent fogging.

PHOTOS: KEN FAUGHT

Moose has solved that problem with waterproof-tape–backed spandex panels. An honorable mention goes to LBZ's baggy riding pants, which, because of their over-the-boot design, keep water out of the top of your boots, while offering good thickness as a layer of protection against body hits.

THE BOTTOM LINE

No matter how warmly you dress, the most important accessory while riding in foul weather is your common sense. We love riding as much—or more—than the next guy and have ridden in some pretty unfavorable conditions, but if the weather is just too damned nasty to ride in, we'll save our bikes and bodies for another day. There's *always* next weekend.

DIRECTORY

ANSWER RACING 805/257-4411
AXO SPORT 800/222-4296
LBZ 714/901-1545
MOOSE RACING 909/428-2424
MSR 909/340-3301
OAKLEY 714/951-0991
SCOTT 208/622-1000
SINISALO 805/257-3386
SMITH SPORT OPTICS 208/726-4477

Double-paned, vented lenses like this Oakley lens work well, but can scratch rather easily. Still, in nonmuddy situations they're hard to beat. Smith also produces a similar lens.

Wraparound hand guards might not look very stylish, but they do an unequaled job of shielding your hands from cold air.

DICK BURLESON ON BRAKING

The AA loop at the *Dirt Rider* 24-hour test (see our May '97 issue) featured a couple of nasty downhills that required efficient use of the front and rear brakes. Simply locking them up wouldn't yield favorable results, as the tight, rocky single-track required more finesse than that. Here's the legendary Dick Burleson to point out the basics of effective braking on steep downhills.

1 "This downhill drops off a ridge, and it's a little rutty because it's in soft dirt," Burleson says. "It's actually a lot steeper than it looks. The first thing you want to do when attacking a downhill this steep is to get your weight way back."

2 "I keep my speed under control by riding the front brake. When the hill is this steep, once you start your way down, you're on your way down. There's no stopping."

3 "Instead of letting off the brakes and trying to slow down suddenly further down the hill, I control my speed right from the top by riding the front brake. Notice how much the fork is compressed; my front brake is doing the majority of the braking. You want to keep your rear wheel spinning; locking up the rear wheel causes you to skid."

4 "Looking ahead is important so that you know what's coming. Brace yourself behind the bar as you apply steady pressure to the front brake. You don't want to stiff-arm the handlebar, though. That doesn't let the fork do its job."

5 "Keeping your hand on the clutch is also important, so that you can keep from stalling the motor."

HOT-WEATHER RIDING TIPS

In a perfect world, we'd do our dirt riding in perfect weather—low humidity and just barely warm enough to wear a jersey. Of course, it would only rain at night, and we'd never be plagued with any dust or deep mud. While those might actually be the conditions encountered when riding in heaven (or Shangri-La), if the rest of us poor earthbound souls waited for conditions that favorable to ride in, it would take a *long* time to wear out a dirt bike. The rude fact is that much of our riding takes place in pestilent heat.

So while the rest of the population parades about in bathing costumes (or loin cloths), we wrap our bodies in nylon, leather, plastic and heat-stamped foam until only our eyes remain free enough to shed heat—and then we cover them with goggles. The saving grace here is that motorcycles move—automatic air conditioning. Also, even though all but the insane or stupid ride fully clothed, we have some great options in riding gear that will help us keep our cool.

While in Florida for our Daytona Motorcycle Week road trip, we checked out the regimens top GNCC and Daytona supercross riders employed to battle the intense heat and humidity.

Suzuki's Rodney Smith has raced European motocross GPs, Qualifiers, GNCC/hare scrambles and ISDE events during his career, in addition to racing motocross professionally in the U.S. and South America. Here, he displays comprehensive preparation for heat. He has an umbrella for shade, a sliced-up jersey to aid cooling airflow, a cool, damp towel around his neck and Lori Hamilton—very effectively distracting his mind from the heat.

While Smith kicks it in the shade, stays cool and prepares mentally for the race, Hamilton packs the bladder of his drink system with as much ice as it will hold, then fills it with a 50/50 mixture of water and Cytomax. Some riders stay with straight water or mix it with other electrolyte-filled sports drinks like Gatorade. This type of drink system has an insulated outer sleeve, so the ice will last. The cold liquid not only quenches thirst and renews fluids, it helps cool the body.

Steve Hatch demonstrates a couple of good points here. Not only is he dressed to stay cool before the race, but he has specially prepared Scott goggles. Bevo Forti from Scott sticks a small slice of a panty-liner minipad to the top foam. (Make sure you buy a brand that uses the absorbent crystals found in baby diapers.) These pads absorb enormous amounts of water and keep goggles from getting sweated out. Hatch also recommends drinking a gallon of water a day for two days before the race, then a half gallon the day of the event—but finish it two hours before the race.

75

PHOTOS: KEN FAUGHT

Nose wheelies have become one of the latest trends in motocross and McGrath is one of the best at the trials-inspired technique that teaches the effective use of the front brake and body positioning. It also shows how the front tire responds to different types of terrain, since nose wheelies require sufficient traction. When traction is not available, the front end will plow or twist, often causing the rider to lose his balance.

Dedicated racers know there's more to training than pounding laps day in and day out. Even the best courses can get boring after a few days. That's why top riders, like four-time supercross champion Jeremy McGrath, mix play riding into their daily routine. Play riding can teach you about your abilities, perception and the bike's reaction to different situations. It also amplifies the fun of riding and will ultimately make you a better rider.

The conventional wheelie is also important. It teaches a rider balance, throttle control and clutch work. A rider will also become more comfortable riding with the front wheel in the air, which is becoming increasingly important with the amount of uphill doubles that comprise today's tracks.

SERIOUS PRACTICE MADE FUN

Modifying a line is sometimes necessary to improve its effectiveness. This can be done with a shovel, by hand or even with the bike itself (by spinning the rear wheel to dig in the line). Here, McGrath is removing some big dirt clods.

Cliff climbs are more important for off-road riders but can teach motocrossers balance, torque, clutch and throttle control, weight distribution, body positioning and traction. Start off small and move to steeper hills. Also, make sure the surrounding area is clear of rocks, trenches, trees or anything that could injure you if you don't make it.

Even though we use the term *play riding*, this is serious practice and shouldn't be attempted alone. In fact McGrath lent a hand as Guy Cooper attempted this cliff climb at Cooper's ranch in Stillwater, Oklahoma. Cooper had two spotters stand at the top, ready to catch him and his bike if he got into trouble. When attempting cliff climbs, leave yourself a way out. Plan an escape route in case things get ugly. In most cases, you should lean into the hill and get away from your bike. Also, be careful that you don't loop out, because this makes it almost impossible to get away from your cartwheeling machine. Just for the record, Cooper finally got it right after four times, boosting his confidence.

Experimenting with midair tricks is an excellent way to learn how to correct the bike in the air when it does the unexpected. The more you understand how your bike handles, the better off you'll be at all times, especially in an emergency.

Practice the same jump over and over to learn how a bike handles and how your suspension responds to different scenarios. One excellent way to learn how to double is to jump to the side of the second obstacle to get your timing right. This won't be possible at all tracks, but it can give you a good idea of trajectory and the amount of speed required to successfully make the leap.

Play riding doesn't have to be limited to jumps; in fact, there's a lot to be learned from playing in turns.

Trade challenges with your friends. McGrath and Jimmy Button spent three days at Cooper's house, and the trio came up with some impressive challenges for one another.

Dicing with your friends is a fantastic way to improve your passing skills. When done safely, it's a good opportunity to learn how to avoid being brake checked and how to use creative lines.

GUY COOPER ON LINE CHOICE

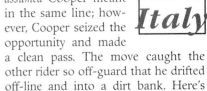

In certain instances you'll encounter a fairly wide area of ridable terrain that has only one good line. Most of the time this won't pose a serious problem, but if you're following a slower rider, it could be potentially hazardous (if the rider were to fall in front of you), or it may open up an opportunity (if you can seek an alternate line to make a pass).

The mind-set for lead riders in one-line areas is that *they* are in control. Most of the time they figure no one will pass them unless it's in an extremely aggressive manner. In this sequence, we set up the rider on the number seven bike and he fell into this "invincible" mental trap. Team USA's ISDE alternate Guy Cooper told the rider that he would follow him through a mud hole. Naturally, the rider *assumed* Cooper meant in the same line; however, Cooper seized the opportunity and made a clean pass. The move caught the other rider so off-guard that he drifted off-line and into a dirt bank. Here's Cooper to explain.

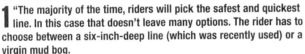

1 "The majority of the time, riders will pick the safest and quickest line. In this case that doesn't leave many options. The rider has to choose between a six-inch-deep line (which was recently used) or a virgin mud bog.

"In order for this maneuver to work, you have to prepare for the opportunity. You won't have a lot of warning. That's why it's important to stick near the rider ahead of you even if you play follow the leader for a while. You must analyze the situation quickly and decide whether the open area poses any danger. In this case it appeared staying clean was the only reason riders weren't taking any other lines."

2 "Be sure you can make the pass. It would be pointless to take an unnecessary risk if you didn't have a decent shot at making it stick. If it doesn't look like you have a realistic shot at beating the other rider to the intersection of the main line, then you have to assess the situation and see if it's really a gamble worth taking. The last thing you want to do is get stuck and be passed by other riders.

"Once I determined I wanted to take another line, I got the best possible drive and wheelied over the water. I didn't want to get wet, because it's easy for your hands to blister with water-soaked gloves."

3 "The other rider finally noticed that I was attempting a pass. By this time, he was totally committed to his line and couldn't do anything safely to block me. Ideally, I would have passed him a few feet earlier and that would have allowed me to splash his goggles and really screw up his concentration."

4 "At this point the pass is made and I will beat him to the intersection. The gamble, though a small one, paid off."

BACK TO BASICS

By Gary Semics

Two important techniques form the foundations on which you develop a correct riding style. These are the proper hand and arm position and the correct foot placement on the pegs. You may already use these techniques but chances are you don't. Learn to do them correctly, and through repetition they'll become automatic.

I taught Jeremy McGrath these two things when I first began to work with him in the mid-'80s, and look where he's taken himself!

To show the importance of the proper hand, arm and foot position, I will analyze my form as I negotiate a flat, sweeping corner.

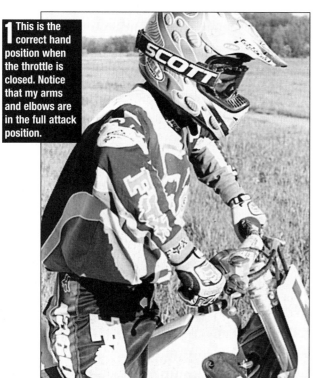

1 This is the correct hand position when the throttle is closed. Notice that my arms and elbows are in the full attack position.

2 This is the correct hand and arm position when the throttle is open. Notice that I maintain the attack position with my elbows—I don't allow them to fall to my sides.

3 If you don't start off with the correct hand position when the throttle is closed, then when you open the throttle, your hand and arm position—as shown here—will limit your ability to move your upper body and compromise leverage.

4 A common mistake is using the arch instead of the ball of the foot on the peg, especially when the rear brake is not being used. You get better feel and control when you use the ball of your foot.

PHOTOS: KEN FAUGHT

5 As I enter the corner, I move from standing to sitting. I'm still on the brakes, and the throttle is closed. Using the correct hand and arm position allows me to move my upper body around and gives me more leverage and throttle control.

6 Now I'm sitting in the corner as I feather off the brakes and employ the clutch and throttle. My body is positioned relatively forward, which helps the rear wheel break loose and drift into the corner.

7 I've made the transition from braking to accelerating. I'm still sliding the rear wheel around, but now it's under power. I've returned my foot from the rear brake to the outside footpeg. I'm on the ball of my foot, but sometimes it's difficult to make this transition quickly. In these cases it's OK to go from the rear brake to the arch of the foot. Just make sure to get back on the ball of your foot as soon as you can.

8 A look from the inside of the same corner reveals my hand and arm are positioned correctly, allowing me to position my upper body well forward. This helps keep the bike sliding and pivoting through the exit of the corner. As soon as I complete the corner, I get the ball of my foot back on the peg. This is the fastest and easiest way around a sweeping corner, and man, does it feel good!

81

SUSPENSION S.O.S.

ORDER OF OPERATION

KNOW YOUR ABCs

By Scott Hoffman

Before you drop a load of cash on suspension revalving, it's best to figure out if such a costly endeavor is necessary. A lot of riders don't bother to follow the proper procedure when it comes to tuning stock or revalved suspension components.

No matter what suspension situation you have, some basic steps must be followed. Suspension tuning is rider specific; each rider has a different style and he or she needs to spend the time to set up the bike accordingly. Even when a suspension tuner revalves components to fit a specific rider's weight, riding ability and the particular type of riding he or she does, the rider still needs to fine-tune the clickers, fork height and spring preload.

The following is not intended to intimidate the average person with long, drawn-out details of the inner workings of valve shims, hydraulics, pop-off valves or other gadgets or gizmos. This is simply our guide to the basics of suspension tuning. We hooked up with Rob Henrickson of RG3 Suspension (714/630-0786) to help compile our suspension tuning primer.

KEN FAUGHT

[FACT] In 1979, plastic motocross boots were introduced by Scott, MXL and Tebo.

UNDERSTANDING SUSPENSION

In a nutshell, suspension works off hydraulic damping, spring force and leverage ratios. The valve shims are a series of small washers stacked together that regulate the flow of oil through a passage, slowing the rate of fork or shock movement. The following is a glossary of the principles.

Valve shims are speed sensitive. The harder the force compressing the shock or fork, the more resistance the valve shim exerts against the oil flow. This is very similar to what happens when you try to run underwater. When you go slow, it is easy to move through the water. But when you try to run, the resistance requires you work harder.

Shock springs are position sensitive. The farther the spring compresses, the stiffer it gets. Because of this, spring rates are not based solely on rider weight, but rather on weight, riding ability and type of riding.

Linkage ratios are graphs of the change in the swingarm's leverage on the shock as the rear wheel travels through its full arc. Traditionally, the farther the wheel moves up in the travel, the quicker the shock compresses. The quicker the shock compresses, the stiffer it gets because of the increased hydraulic resistance on the valve shims.

Stiction is usually associated with the fork. The union between the inner tubes and the outer tubes through the bushing contacts creates stiction. Stiction, and binding, occur when the tubes flex and create further resistance. This force affects suspension action. Unfortunately, this is unavoidable with current telescoping fork designs.

GLOSSARY OF PRINCIPLES

BASICS

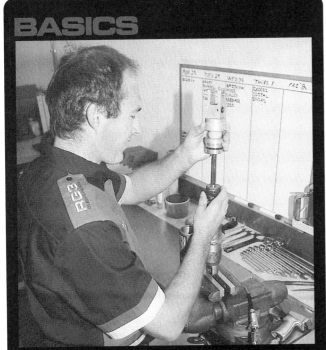

Servicing suspension is like changing the oil in the transmission or replacing a top end: If it's not done on schedule, it will affect the performance of the bike. It's important to understand that an oil change and a complete service are two different procedures. The folks at RG3 actually do a complete rebuild on the shock and the fork. They inspect and replace any worn parts including bent, worn or broken valve shims, seals, bushings and piston bands. If there is a broken or excessively worn part in a shock or fork, a simple oil change will not fix the problem.

TOOLS

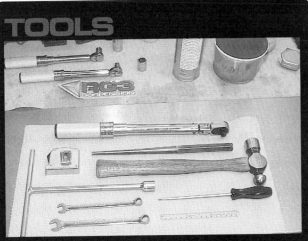

Having the proper tools is crucial, and for the record, a pair of locking pliers, a three-inch screwdriver and grandpa's old ball peen hammer will *not* suffice. Build a motorcycle-only toolbox that goes wherever your bike goes. For suspension tuning the following tools will make life easy:
· Dead-blow hammer
· 12-inch flat-end punch
· Eight-inch-long straight-blade screwdriver. The tip should fit well into compression and rebound clickers in the fork and shock as well as the air bleed screw in the fork.
· Measuring tape, preferably in millimeters, or a suspension-sag measuring tool
· Fork oil level gauge specific to the make and model of your bike
· 8, 10 and 12mm box-end wrenches to check front-end alignment
· 14mm T-handle for adjusting high-speed compression when applicable
· A pad of paper and pen to document settings
· Torque wrench with the proper socket and/or hex head to properly torque triple-clamp fasteners
· Small machinist-style scale (in millimeters)

BACK TO BASICS

If you are starting with a new bike, break in the suspension before testing or tuning suspension components. You might want to measure and adjust the bike sag if it seems extremely off the mark, but don't spend too much time because it may change slightly. Check the front axle alignment to ensure the forks are not bound up. Inspect and torque fork triple-champ bolts and check remaining nuts and bolts throughout the bike. Ride at an easy pace for 30 to 60 minutes. This will usually offer ample time to break in suspension components.

If the bike is used, it's a good idea to determine when the suspension was last serviced. Old worn-out internal parts and oil can affect suspension action. It would be a shame to spend an entire day testing suspension settings only to find out the fork and shock were not working properly.

Make sure the rear wheel is fully extended before taking measurements.

SETTING RACE SAG

Before a rider changes clickers, race sag or rider sag should be established first. Race sag is the measurable difference between the rear axle and rear fender when the rear wheel is off the ground compared to when the rider is in full gear on the bike. Check with your owner's manual for the recommended setting. This is the best starting point. There is no magic number that works with every rider. Sag is a matter of preference and testing is the only way to find the best setting. A rider may start with the recommended setting and tighten or loosen the spring one or two turns until the best setting is achieved.

Start by placing the bike on a stand. Be sure the rear wheel is off the ground and the bike is not sitting on the linkage. Then measure the distance from the rear axle to the rear fender using a measuring tape or sag gauge. Mark the fender to make sure the measuring area is the same. Always use the rear axle as the start of your measurement. For the most accurate measurement, sit the rider—in full gear—on the bike. If possible, have a third person hold the bike so the rider can rest both feet on the pegs.

When measuring race sag, remember that too much sag will give a soft feel in small bumps while causing the shock to ride too low in the stroke in larger bumps, resulting in a harsh feeling. The bike may be a little more stable at speed, but excess sag will affect the bike's turning ability.

Not enough sag, on the other hand, can cause the bike to turn too quickly and become unstable, especially when a rider rolls off the gas. This can also transmit a harsh feeling through small bumps.

When you find the optimal setting, jot down the measurements and write down basic notes on how the bike performed with different sag settings.

SPRING RATES

Having the correct spring rates can affect bike setup. Spring rates can rely on personal preference to a degree, but they are usually affected by rider weight and ability. For the most part, a bike comes from the factory set up for a rider in the 150-170 pound range. Riders under that weight may need softer springs, while heavier riders may benefit from stiffer springs.

Fork springs that are too soft can cause a diving effect. In this case, the fork sits low in the travel and may bottom too easily. Unfortunately, there is no real way to accurately test sag in the fork because of stiction. If the race sag is set correctly in the rear but there is no free sag, the spring is usually too soft.

Free sag is how much the bike settles while standing on its own and the shock is topped out, without any free play when you lift the rear fender. Around

RACE SAG

2

Using a measuring tape or a sag scale (left), take the first readings with the bike on a stand. Mark a reference point on the fender for consistent measurements.

For best results, have a third person hold the bike so the rider can place both feet on the pegs (below).

3

40mm or more of free sag in the rear is a sign the shock spring may be too stiff. When the race sag is set correctly, the shock should have between 10 and 40mm of free sag.

FORK POSITION

In direct relation to rear sag is the fork's height in the triple clamps. Once a rider has found a comfortable rear sag setting, he or she should tweak fork height to balance the bike and find the best turning-versus-stability compromise. Slight changes in fork height position can affect handling, suspension action and stability. Your toolbox should have a small machinist-type scale to set fork height. Fork position changes should be made in 2mm to 5mm increments.

If the fork tubes are pushed too far up in the clamps, the bike may feel unstable at speed and knife in too much in corners. Conversely, if the fork tubes are too low in the clamps, the bike becomes very stable at speed but sacrifices turning ability.

After you have set fork height, you may retest rear sag positions. Remember, these settings are based on rider preference and feel. Write down the

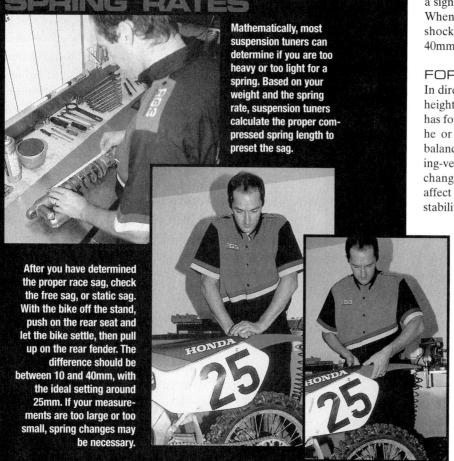

SPRING RATES

Mathematically, most suspension tuners can determine if you are too heavy or too light for a spring. Based on your weight and the spring rate, suspension tuners calculate the proper compressed spring length to preset the sag.

After you have determined the proper race sag, check the free sag, or static sag. With the bike off the stand, push on the rear seat and let the bike settle, then pull up on the rear fender. The difference should be between 10 and 40mm, with the ideal setting around 25mm. If your measurements are too large or too small, spring changes may be necessary.

best settings for future reference. At this point the bike should be well balanced between the fork and shock.

COMPRESSION CLICKERS

The compression adjuster is located on the shock reservoir on top of the shock. Fork compression adjusters differ depending on what fork you might have. Almost all forks, with the exception of late-model Showa forks, have the compression adjusters on the bottom of the fork. Check your owner's manual to verify clicker locations. Rebound adjusters are usually located on the bottom of the shock. Other shocks may have a dial right above the lower attachment point and below the shock spring.

Start off by setting your clickers to the stock positions. Refer to your owner's manual if you are unsure of the settings. Most clickers are counted counterclockwise from all the way in. Again, write down the starting settings for quick reference.

Ride the bike and get a feel for how the rear end is absorbing little stuff and if it is too stiff and harsh. If there is a harsh feeling on small and medium bumps, try going out on the compression adjuster. One or two clicks can make a big difference.

If the bike feels soft and mushy and bottoms too easily, try going in on the adjuster. Adjust only one clicker at a time unless the bike is heavily unbalanced. Once you have a good feel for the rear end, move on to the fork.

The same procedure applies for the fork. Go out and ride the bike to get a feel for how the fork behaves. Is the fork absorbing bumps and braking bumps? Is it transmitting harshness through the handlebar? If so, soften up the clickers. If the fork feels mushy and bottoms easily, go in on the compression adjuster.

HIGH-SPEED COMPRESSION

This is a very confusing element of suspension tuning, even for some seasoned riders. Understand that the high-speed adjuster affects shock shaft speed and the damping created by shaft speed, but does not necessarily affect bike speed, although the two may be related. High-speed damping affects sharp-edge bumps, some big, fast hits and hard, flat landings.

REBOUND CLICKERS

This is another place to begin with stock settings. Rebound clickers can be very

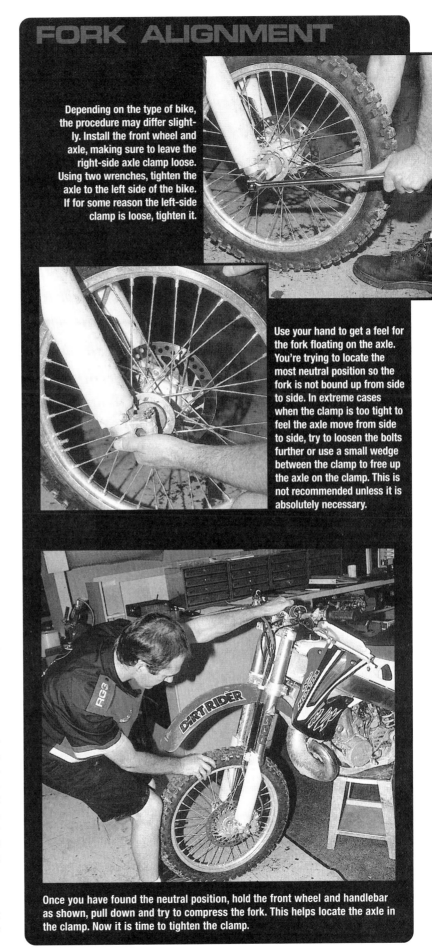

FORK ALIGNMENT

Depending on the type of bike, the procedure may differ slightly. Install the front wheel and axle, making sure to leave the right-side axle clamp loose. Using two wrenches, tighten the axle to the left side of the bike. If for some reason the left-side clamp is loose, tighten it.

Use your hand to get a feel for the fork floating on the axle. You're trying to locate the most neutral position so the fork is not bound up from side to side. In extreme cases when the clamp is too tight to feel the axle move from side to side, try to loosen the bolts further or use a small wedge between the clamp to free up the axle on the clamp. This is not recommended unless it is absolutely necessary.

Once you have found the neutral position, hold the front wheel and handlebar as shown, pull down and try to compress the fork. This helps locate the axle in the clamp. Now it is time to tighten the clamp.

FORK POSITION

Fork height is often overlooked, but be aware it is a valuable tool to dial in the suspension and overall handling of a bike.

tricky. For example, it's tempting to blame rear-end kicking on rebound. However, this symptom may be a sign the bike is riding too low in the stroke or the compression is too stiff, causing the wheel to deflect off bumps. This is exactly why a rider should only adjust one clicker at a time. Start with the obvious first and go one or two clicks in or out to offset the symptoms. Ride the bike and see if the problem has been solved or worsened. Make further changes if things are improving; go the opposite direction if they are getting worse.

Fork rebound can be very difficult to adjust. The average rider should stick close to stock settings unless there is an obvious problem. Symptoms such as the fork packing up in braking bumps are a sign the fork rebound may be too slow.

FORK OIL HEIGHT

Fork oil height is another tool used to tune forks. When you adjust the fork oil height you are basically adjusting the air spring in the fork. (Air spring is the compression of the excess air space in the upper quadrant of a fork.) The higher the fork oil height, the stiffer the air spring makes the fork action in the latter part of the stroke. If you lower the fork oil height, fork action is softened, but the bike becomes more susceptible to bottoming. Be advised that some forks, such as the twin-chamber Suzuki fork, do not go by fork oil height but rather by volume. Refer to the owner's manual for the maximum and minimum oil height or volume.

WHEEL POSITION

The rear wheel can affect the suspension and the handling of the bike depending on its position in the swingarm. Because of this, be sure to recheck sag settings whenever wheel position is altered.

The farther back the wheel, the better the high-speed stability of the bike. The farther forward the wheel, the better the traction—at the cost of high-speed stability. When the wheel is back, shock action can become softer due to added leverage. The opposite occurs when the wheel is moved forward.

It's also critical that the fork is properly aligned with the front axle. A misaligned fork can cause excessive wear to bushings, poor fork action and a poor handling bike. Adjustments should be done with the bike on a stand with little pressure on the front wheel.

HELPFUL HINTS

- Make only one adjustment at a time.
- Keep a record of adjustments and how they affect the bike's handling.
- Periodically check race sag to ensure the measurements have not changed because of shock spring fatigue.
- Check race sag after major wheel adjustments or sprocket changes.
- Service the fork and shock on a regular basis.
- While your suspension is being serviced, place an O-ring on the fork tubes and the shock shaft, or use a zip-tie on the fork leg. This helps determine if you are using the entire stroke of the fork at a given track.
- Inspect and lube the steering head and linkage on a regular basis.
- Have someone videotape or watch you ride to determine if the bike is having any visual handling problems.

If you have ever found yourself in this position because your suspension pitched you off the bike, laminate this story and keep it in your toolbox for reference.

DEEP BREATHS...

Suspension tuning, if not performed properly, can be a hair-raising experience. Bear in mind that when you change settings on the fork, the shock is affected and vice versa. If the bike feels soft everywhere, start by stiffening up the compression on the shock, ride the bike, and if the shock feels better, try balancing the bike by stiffening up the fork as well.

If you get lost in your settings, go back to the stock settings and start over. Henrickson believes that the owner's manual

can be helpful with troubleshooting, but some manuals can be confusing. He also says that a reputable suspension tuner can give advice based on symptoms. Really understanding suspension takes time and experience. For the most part, the clickers should not be too far off the standard factory settings. If you have covered every possible scenario and are still having problems getting your bike's suspension working, consult a suspension tuner for possible further internal modifications.

[FACT] In 1989, Honda rider Chuck Miller won the opening round of the AMA National Hare & Hound series in Lucerne Valley, California.

Hand guards are an invaluable jack-of-all-trades item, not only in muddy conditions but also if a track or trail is littered with rocks, bushes or trees. You and your hands will be thankful when it comes time to break out the hand guards. In fact, carry two pairs because you know your buddy won't have a pair and you can sell them for top dollar, or you can let him borrow the pair so you don't have to hear the whining.

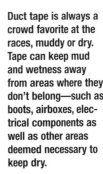

Duct tape is always a crowd favorite at the races, muddy or dry. Tape can keep mud and wetness away from areas where they don't belong—such as boots, airboxes, electrical components as well as other areas deemed necessary to keep dry.

PREPARE FOR MUDDY DAYS

Ever have one of those riding days where you're all excited, your gear bags are packed, the bikes are ready and you're en route to the races or a favorite riding spot when all of a sudden, small droplets of water start to clutter the windshield? The next thing you realize, it's raining cats and dogs, and you have nothing but vented gear packed. This is one example why a rider should always carry a rainy-day kit prepped with the essentials for mud riding, especially during the rainy season. An emergency kit won't bog down your normal effort and can easily fit into a small crate or container.

Having an umbrella, a plastic raincoat with a hood and a water-resistant enduro jacket is priceless on a day of gloom and moisture. The plastic raincoat should have a home in your gear bag at all times.

Keeping as much mud off the bike is key to riding through the muck. Several top mechanics stuff foam into areas where mud gathers. Coarse foam with large holes works best because it doesn't trap water. Foam from a race car's fuel cell or the type that's typically used under skid plates is primo. Carry a few extra pieces in your gear bag or emergency mud kit.

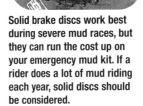

Solid brake discs work best during severe mud races, but they can run the cost up on your emergency mud kit. If a rider does a lot of mud riding each year, solid discs should be considered.

Always keep a few worn-out goggle lenses for a rainy day. Tape the lens to the front of your visor; when excess roost starts to fly your way, all you need to do is tilt your head down. Also notice this rider has taped pieces of an air filter to his helmet to keep mud from sticking to the top of his lid. The air filter could have been spared if the rider had been prepared with an emergency mud pack.

Take a tip from some factory mechanics for that full-factory look. Hold on to a few old inner tubes. Then when it is rainy, halve a tube down the middle and place the pieces over the rear and front tires to keep them dry and free from mud before the start of a race. You will have to remove the wheels to place the tube over the tire. Right before the race starts the tubes can simply be cut off the tires.

A few other items that can possibly help during a muddy day: an extra helmet liner, goggles with Smith Roll Off's and tear-offs, watercraft-style gloves, small hand towels that can attach to riding pants and nonstick cooking spray to coat your bike before a race or ride.

PRO RIDING SECRETS

DESTRY ABBOTT

SAND WASHES WITH HIGH-SPEED TURNS

BY MARK KARIYA

Different dirt riders consider sand washes either heaven or hell. On the one hand, they're often the desert equivalent to a twisty trail in the woods and let you get into a rhythm. On the other hand, many riders have trouble making turns in loose sand so they slow down, which only exacerbates the problem.

Obviously, one of the problems is maintaining speed in sand, but Team Green's Destry Abbott has some suggestions on how to keep it. As the defending AMA National Hare & Hound Champion, the Arizona resident is intimately familiar with sand washes and how to get through them as quickly as possible.

So follow his advice, and you should find yourself in heaven the next time you hit a similar section in the dez.

1 This is the view approaching the turn. This sand wash is flat and smooth, as it's been little-traveled. Ahead to the left is a bend that will have to be dealt with—that's going to be the focus of this tip.

2 "I usually like to stand up [approaching the turn]," Abbott begins, "because in desert racing you don't really know what the corner's going to do—if it's going to make a V or it's going to be fast and gradual. As I enter it, I'm trying to look ahead." Being able to absorb the shock from hidden rocks with your legs is another factor.

4 "You want to stay more to the outside because that's where the berm is, if there's any," Abbott continues. (That wall on the outside doesn't count; there's a small berm built up if you look closer.) "As you're going around the corner, keep your finger on the clutch because you don't know if the corner's going to make a sudden turn or whatever."

3 "As soon as I'm into the corner, then I sit down and power through the corner because then it gets your suspension dug in there," he says. "Motocrossers stand up a lot. [Travis] Pastrana, for instance, would stand up probably around the whole corner, but in off-road we can't do that because we'd waste so much energy. You've got to try to save energy and sit down when you can in the flat, easy stuff. That's what I would do in the corner where it's smooth, and you can sit down and relax. Keep your elbows up in attack mode. Stick your [inside] foot out—not extended all the way—in case you have to dab."

5 Though he is fairly far forward on the bike in the beginning of the turn, Abbott slides back when exiting under power and brings his foot back up to the peg, all of which helps transfer weight rearward. "With a 500, you want to get all the power to the ground that you can," he says.

HOW TO

HANDLE WHOOPS

BY MARK KARIYA

Whoops come in all shapes, sizes and patterns, but their common theme is that they can quickly wear you out. In addition, getting out of shape and crashing at speed isn't too much fun either.

Team Green's Destry Abbott has seen uncounted miles of whoops of all descriptions. As the defending AMA National Hare & Hound Champion, he's naturally developed his own techniques for tackling whoops, and he was kind enough to share these with us through a section of high-speed, fairly large, irregularly spaced ones. They're unlike supercross whoops where, if you've got the suspension, skill and *huevos* to do so, you can basketball them.

Follow along, practice the techniques the next time you come to some whoops and watch your confidence—and speed—increase. It'll help if you can have a buddy watch you and offer instant feedback or videotape you for later viewing. Either way, work up to increased speed a step at a time. You'll find your personal limits expanded in no time.

1 "This stuff's hard; it's physically demanding because you're moving so much on the bike," Abbott begins. "I usually try to wheelie a lot of the [whoops]. If it's a bigger whoop, I try to wheelie it and in the smaller stuff, just try to skim the tops. As long as you can see a ways up [the trail], I try to make some of the big whoops into doubles if I can see the down side [holds no dangers like boulder fields or washouts]. You don't want to jump something where you don't know what you're jumping into. I usually try to stay to the left or the right of these kinds of trails because a lot of riders will ride in the middle, where it's the deepest."

3 "Try to stay relaxed, like anything," Abbott also insists. "In stuff like this you don't want to be too aggressive or you'll jump into [the face of] another one. If [that happens] and you're ready to case it, try to keep your front wheel high. That way you just hit at the top."

2 "Try to keep your body positioned in the middle where you're not having to pull or to push [the handlebar]. That way the bike's rocking back and forth and the seat almost hits your butt, but you're really not using a lot of energy [as you would be if you were] pushing or pulling."

4 Abbott prefers to wheelie into the face of big whoops when he doesn't want to jump too far. "Then you soak it up so you don't jump [too far]," he says. "A lot of times you want to get your front wheel to the top of it and use your back end to soak it up, use your legs—you'll see the seat hit my butt a lot of times—but that way you stay low to the ground and keep your momentum going. You don't want to jump into whoops because then you case them or you land in the middle of one, and it just kicks you really hard. I'll keep my foot on the rear brake and drag that." That helps keep the bike straight, reducing the chance of swapping.

DOING THE DAB

BY MARK KARIYA

It's best to keep your feet on the pegs whenever possible since doing so makes it harder for logs, rocks or other trail debris to get at them. However, there are times to disregard this rule.

As six-time AMA National Enduro Champion Randy Hawkins picks his way through this slow, rocky trail, he's sitting as he rounds a tight turn. Exiting the turn, he throws his inside leg forward, aiming for a rock to plant it on.

"I use this to give myself a little leverage and actually push off from the rock," he reveals. This is especially useful if one of the tires hits a small, loose rock which rolls out from underneath and temporarily upsets the balance.

Just as trials riders sometimes dab deliberately, those who ride regular machinery can benefit from a well-placed or -timed footplant. Just be sure to get those feet back on the pegs as soon as possible.

As Randy Hawkins comes out of this slow turn, he really can't be on the pegs because of the trees. Yet the loose rocks littering the trail make for an unpredictable balance. Thus, he throws his inside foot out and deliberately dabs in order to maintain balance, pushing off as he rides away. Rest assured, though, that he'll get his foot back on the peg in short order to reduce the chances of smashing it.

PRO **RIDING**

TIM FERRY, RICKY CARMICHAEL AND KEVIN WINDHAM

DEEP **RUTTED TRACKS**

BY SCOTT HOFFMAN

Deep, thick dirt carved up by more wheel-sucking ruts than the rain-soaked front line of a WWI battlefield, does it sound appealing? For most riders, deep rutted tracks are a nightmare; having to ride a slot car–style course can be very frustrating, not to mention physically demanding. The principal problem is just plain lack of familiarity. Often a deeply rutted track is the result of rain or a course that has been ripped deep and overwatered. Because it is hard to prepare for this situation, it is a good idea to know a few survival tricks.

First off, never look directly down at the rut or line you're riding through. As soon as a pilot fixes on the rut directly below, it causes him to oversteer, often throwing him off-balance and/or having him cross-rut and go down. Always look ahead, pick a line and ride through the rut instead of trying to steer through a line. Keep the bike driving forward to some degree when not braking. It is harder to negotiate through ruts when the power is off. When the bike is driving forward, that keeps the front wheel lighter and helps keep the machine tracking in a straight line. Use body English to steer the bike as much as possible; shifting body weight from side to side keeps the bike balanced. In deep rutted turns, keep your outside leg on the peg, riding on the ball of your foot. Your inside leg should be leading out front and off the dirt to avoid snagging the heel of your boot. Never follow a rider into the same rut. If for some reason the front-runner stalls, crashes or bobbles, it is very difficult to change lines quickly. And finally, try to avoid the deepest ruts on the track. Some ruts are so deep that footpegs, front fork and rear swingarm drag in the dirt and often stop a rider dead in his tracks. These few tips can make a huge difference when these conditions surface from the depths of the earth.

1 Tim Ferry's four-stroke tractors through ruts because of its torquey power delivery, although in this shot Ferry made a slight mistake that forced him to dab his foot for correction. You want to avoid dabbing whenever possible. The dirt in this shot was very thick and mushy; it is very easy to catch a boot and twist an ankle or knee in these conditions. Because Ferry is such a talented rider his outstretched leg hardly affected his drive from the turn. Although if the boot had dug in the dirt, that could have lifted him off the seat and caused his body to rotate, throwing off his balance.

2 Instead of dropping into the deep peg-dragging rut, Ricky Carmichael is searching for alternative lines that will pose less of a threat. This line he chose, although smoother, turned out to be slower than charging through the rut to his left. RC was forced to brake harder and scrub off more speed to go to the extreme inside. An equally fast line developed at this point but not until the second moto. This is a prime example of why it is a good idea to always keep an eye out for alternative lines.

3 Notice Kevin Windham's body position in this shot: his peg is digging into the ground so hard that it is forcing his bike upright. To counter the effect, K-Dub is using body English to balance the bike so it does not stand up and cause him to high side. As you can see, he is forcing the bike over to keep it in the line; he could have slowed down but then he would have lost his drive out of the turn.

MAINTAIN DRIVE WITH STANDING WHEELIES

BY MARK KARIYA

Wheelies aren't just for clowning around or showing off. They can be immensely useful tools in any dirt rider's arsenal. Suzuki's Steve Hatch proved so when he demonstrated along this portion of trail near his Arizona home, a place where he practices regularly to hone his GNCC skills.

In this example, Hatch finds two bumps in the trail. They're not large enough or close enough to double jump, and hitting them separately as most people would do definitely would throw him in the air twice, resulting in lost momentum and wasted energy.

So he simply stands up and wheelies from one to the other.

That helps keep his rear tire hooked up, resulting in more speed as he accelerates and greater braking control as he approaches the next turn.

"If I just hit it fast, it would kick," Hatch insists. "The front end would jump up, the back end would jump up, then I'd go down into the [valley between bumps] and I'd hit the bank on the far side, which would throw me back up in the air. When you're in the air, you can't brake or get ready for the corner.

"Therefore, I just make it one smooth [action] where my rear tire never leaves the ground between the corner, [the first bump,] the [following] dip and the second little mound."

1 Here's what the obstacle looks like as you'd approach it. As Hatch comes out of the corner, two sizable bumps spaced quite a ways apart lie in his path on the trail. "Normally, if I was racing, I'd be in second gear coming out of the corner," he begins. "Instead, since I'm going to wheelie all the way to the far bank, I put it in third so it's more tractable. The dip [after the first bump] kind of goes down after [the first bump] so [using] second, when it hits the powerband, it'd want to wheelie over backward."

2 "Just pull back in kind of a small wheelie to begin with because of the drop-off [on the other side of the first bump], then that brings it up again. You really have to know your bike and practice standing wheelies; that's the main thing," he points out.

3 "I'm using a lot of muscle control here, because if I don't have the front end high enough, I can pull back with my arms," Hatch continues. "Or if it's too high, I can just let off the throttle or pull in the clutch a little."

4 "I want the front wheel to land just on the top of the second bump so when it does, it actually deadens the blow of the bump and that drives the rear end through it," he says. "If I land [the front wheel] too soon, like I did a couple of times, it'll hit the front end on [the bump] and pop the rear end up. If I go too far, that's not good either because then I'm hitting the bump with the rear end before the front end's down. When you hit that bump [correctly] with the front and back [simultaneously], once that front compresses, it keeps it from bumping the rear end up. If you hit it too far [past the bump], it gets air and then compresses your suspension. You're actually using it to pivot the bike and let it soak [up the jolts] all the way through."

NIGHT ADVICE

BY MARK KARIYA

You can ride all day and night if you wanted to— assuming it's legal in your riding area or that you have no responsibilities which would prevent you from riding just about as much as you want. All it takes is a headlight and the ability to adapt to a strange, new world because even places where you've ridden for years take on a new persona in the dark.

"Riding at night's one of my favorite things to do because it's so different," three-time Baja 1000 winner Johnny Campbell declares.

"Your lights are your world; that's all you're concerned about. When riding in the day, you can see things off in the distance, things that you wouldn't be able to see at night. It's kind of neat because sometimes you don't want to see everything that's going on out there!"

Ten-time Baja 1000 winner Larry Roeseler agrees, "I've always liked it." However, he believes, "The higher concentration level is much harder on you mentally." At least it is when you're trying to do 100 mph through a moonless Mexican night in the middle of nowhere.

In addition to having the lights on your bike and great concentration, keen vision is a requirement for nighttime raging. "We talked a lot about it [at Team Green]," Roeseler recalls. "We always felt the reason Danny Hamel could go so fast in the desert was because he had good eyesight, and that's a factor when you're doing 90 mph in whoops."

As in every facet of the sport, there are some things you need to know or do in order to enjoy it more. The following are a few of the key points.

AFTER DUSK: Riding at night is a great way to get more riding in, whether to spite those short winter days or to escape the daytime heat of summer.

1 You don't need to have a big Baja double-light setup or one of the trick HID (high-intensity discharge) lights to ride at night—although the more light the better. "I tend to adjust the light [to aim] a little on the high side so when I brake, it doesn't shine down too low," Team Green's Larry Roeseler says. "But I've got to be careful when I accelerate because then it can aim too high." That, of course, brings us to the most important tip of all: be smooth. "A smoother technique or riding style is definitely in order at night," Roeseler emphasizes. "You can't ride like you're motoing with sudden acceleration and braking because your lights'll be all over the place, and you can't see."

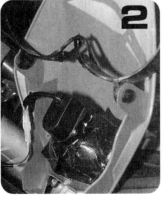

2 Enduro Engineering's Alan Randt reveals a little secret of the stock headlight on a KTM E/XC: They have high and low beams but come wired to power only low. The solution is to pull the connector off the low-beam post and plug it into the high-beam one. Also, Randt suggests taping the area around the reflector housing in back of the headlight shell so light doesn't leak back glaringly into your eyes but instead is concentrated out and forward where it belongs.

3 Actually, having a smaller, less powerful light in tighter trails isn't too much of a liability because you're not going as fast. As Honda's Campbell says, "If you're riding some trails, and you have a smaller light that's closer in [with its beam], it fills in the holes closer to your bike better when you're going over a jump or rise. You can go a bit faster [on trails] with a light that's close in. If you've got something like a big Baja light that's projected to be way out there so you can average a higher speed, it's dark for a longer time when you go over rises, making it a little hairy."

4 Campbell, who's won plenty of races in Baja, knows what it's like to spend countless hours riding through the black of night with nothing but his lamp on his bike to lead his way. JC likes to keep his weight forward—at least during the day. "If you're riding at high speeds and you have a big light system, there's a little more weight on the front end so you ride back on the bike a little more," he says. "I generally ride pretty straight up and down when I'm trying to see a long ways out; I still stand up and ride forward."

5 Another thing Campbell does more at night is use the rear brake: "I probably use a little too much rear brake at night; I drag it a lot. It's just like a security blanket." Riding the rear brake tends to keep the front end on the ground more and the bike a bit more stable, both of which help position the beam where you need it most: on the ground in front of you. The only reason he runs this heavily finned billet-aluminum rear caliper is because "I have a heavy-footed partner [Tim Staab]," Campbell jokes.

6 Campbell also insists, "Riding at night, sometimes you can go faster in sections than you can in the day because of the shadows: You can see rocks or anything in the road or the trail a lot better. Your lights cast a shadow on that obstacle, so it's usually easier to avoid. In the daytime, the light washes things out, so you can't tell where the rocks are—they're the same color as the dirt or sand—and you end up hitting them." As this photo in flat, midday light demonstrates, daylight doesn't always reveal rocks or other obstacles that can jump out and bite you.

STOP THE MADNESS!

Learn to become a better rider

before

after

SCOTT **HOFFMAN**
AND THE **DIRT RIDER**
STAFF
STORY

"Only you can make yourself faster!"

PHOTOS: SCOTT HOFFMAN

ired of being slow, called a goon and getting dirt kicked in your face? If you answered yes, we may have the key to happiness you've long been waiting for. This is not one of those get-rich-quick schemes or a special pill that claims to give you the looks of Brad Pitt and the speed of Ricky Carmichael—although with a little hard work and dedication, the road to quicker lap times is right around the corner. We also won't bamboozle you with a charge of $19.95 for the next 50 months or a claim that "for less than $3.99 the program is completely paid for."

Riding motocross or off-road is grossly misunderstood by those who have never really experienced it. They often make comments like, "How can you be so sore? To drive [ride] a bike you just sit on the seat and turn the gas lever [throttle]." It is difficult to even start to explain to a nonbeliever the magnitude of actions and reactions, both physical and mental, it takes to ride above the very beginning levels. Learning to control throttle and brakes and how to start and stop takes about a day. From that point on, the learning curve is almost infinite. Even riders such as Ricky Carmichael and Jeremy McGrath still practice and seek out new and improved ways to develop into superior riders.

In this piece we will cover techniques that will help the green rider as well as the seasoned veteran. Just remember that it is never too late to learn.

THEORY

When someone first starts to ride, every action is a conscious decision of remembering to pull in the clutch when stopping, use the brakes to stop and slowly let the clutch out while applying the throttle to start. Over time these actions become second nature. A rider starts to build a library of techniques, like how a computer stores information. The more techniques a rider can master and wire into his or her brain, the better a rider he or she becomes. The problem is that some can develop skills and become fairly fast and efficient riders, but their overall technique is flawed with bad habits and poor style. Without correcting the erroneous behavior that have long been seated in the brain, a rider's ability to excel past a certain point is stifled. Sheer natural talent is as rare as a four-leaf clover; that is why us common folk have to work at becoming better riders. Lots of practice while consciously correcting bad habits is the only way to rectify our speed-sucking hang-ups. This is not something that happens overnight; it takes months and possibly years to correct any ingrained behavior. Attending a riding school or private instruction is another great tool to help pinpoint trouble spots. Correcting poor practices can be as difficult as a smoker trying to kick his vice. However, the payoff is worth the effort. Not only will you become a better rider, you will also become a safer one.

Bubba Stewart (259) is slated to become the next superstar in the sport of motocross and supercross. Observe his near perfect riding style: leg extended off the ground, elbows up, finger on the clutch and he is looking out front to predict his next move.

Once a rider has mastered the basics of riding, it is time to learn the first, and sometimes the most important, technique: body position.

BODY POSITION

Body position, or what some instructors refer to as the attack position, is the hub from which the rider works. But becoming a better pilot goes beyond knowing how to be aggressive, it means

STARTS

According to Donnie Hansen and a host of other instructors, practicing starts should always be part of your training regimen. For cement starts, Hansen recommends you keep as much weight as possible on the rear wheel to improve traction on the slippery surface. If the cement is really slick, heating up the tire via a burnout can aid grip. Control of the clutch and throttle is most critical, and 0–125cc bikes should start in first gear while 250cc-plus bikes should start in second. Chirping the rear tire before a start will help you get a feel for the amount of traction the ground offers, so when the gate drops for real, you know the perfect combination of clutch and throttle to launch the bike off the grid. For dirt starts, you should move forward on the seat and keep your head over the handlebar. This helps control the front wheel to keep it from lofting up at the start; on dirt starts you can put a lot more power to the ground when the gate drops.

Pick your starting gate wisely. If possible, choose a gate nearest to the first turn, yet not too close to the outside of either side of the gate. Five to eight gated from the center, nearest to the first turn is best. Hansen also insists his students attend the riders' meeting so they understand the starting procedure; different tracks may alter the process. Watch the races before your event to get an idea when the gate might drop.

Then when the gate drops, pull your feet up on the pegs as soon as possible to avoid missing a shift point. A split second delay can make the difference between a holeshot or a mid-pack start.

Just remember starts are the one place a rider can pass 40 riders in less than 100 yards.

learning to maintain the proper body position whether that be attack or neutral or in between. This alertness allows a rider to prepare for almost any obstacle, whether on the trail or at the motocross track. It also makes it easier to take an evasive action in the event of an unexpected bike change. If a rider is too far back or forward on the bike, hitting an unseen rock or square-edged bump can easily eject him in a split second. That's when staying neutral on the bike is the best defense.

Gary Bailey instructs students at his motocross school to start off by trying to keep their knees above or slightly behind the footpegs. Bailey says that because the bike pivots off of the footpegs front to back and side to side, keeping the rider's weight centered over the bike works best. He also says that when a rider lets his knees ride in front of the pegs this causes the rear end to become loose. Watching pros like Ricky Carmichael, Jeremy McGrath or Travis Pastrana is the best way to understand this theory.

With the legs in position, the rest of the body should follow suit. The knees and arms should be slightly bent. Bailey notes that the proper arm position should resemble doing a push-up on the handlebar. For the most part, the upper body should be kept over the front of the bike. There are times when sitting upright is necessary to get traction in the mud and/or deep sand, although a rider should try to maintain forward momentum via projecting his or her bike forward whenever possible. Bailey credits McGrath for bringing this concept into

SITTING ATTACK POSITION

DAVI MILLSAPS WITH GARY BAILEY

STANDING ATTACK POSITION

the sport. MC was one of the first racers to project his body forward, similar to riding a BMX bike. Before his era racers often rode more to the back of the motorcycle, but because of today's front suspension technology, this is no longer necessary. MC throws his body forward into jumps and then lets the bike come up and rotate under him. This shoots him forward and not as high compared to other racers.

Gripping the handlebar is another important aspect of rider position. It works best to let the grip ride diagonal in the palm, similar to holding a tennis racket. This helps transfer the force from the lower outside of the palm to the inside of the hand between the forefinger and thumb. This grip also helps keep your wrist straighter. And try not to ride holding the bar too tightly—that is unless the

terrain really calls for it—as this will cause arm-pump and premature exhaustion, especially during long races or rides.

Bailey encourages students to ride on the balls of their feet as much as possible. If you watch the top professional racers, notice how often the pros shift their feet on the pegs. This is very important for off-road riding, especially in areas where there are exposed rocks and stumps. You don't want to catch the toe of your boot on a planted rock while going 30 mph; it's not pretty. Riding on the balls of your feet allows you to feel more movement under the bike and it is a lot easier to shift weight from side to side. Be careful when landing off jumps with your feet too far back on the pegs. Bailey says it is possible as long as you absorb the landing with your legs. On small jumps we have found that it works well, but for anything over 20 feet, we prefer landing with the boots centered on the pegs.

Turning a motorcycle, like almost any action on a motorcycle, starts with proper body position. Mike Healey's motocross school works with

TURNING TECHNIQUES

dozens of racers and stresses that turning a motorcycle is based on body position and transferring as much weight forward as possible. Healey says you should look ahead to pinpoint what is the best and fastest line. Because

ricky CARMICHAEL

PHOTOS: SCOTT HOFFMAN

97

tracks change so rapidly, the same line that worked during practice may not be the line that is best during the race. This is why it is very important to study the course before or during the opening laps of a race.

Hitting the proper braking points for turns can make or break a race. Healey likes to teach his students to start braking a little "early" to better set up for the turn. If you are still on the brakes going into the apex of a turn, the bike will have lost most of its momentum at that point. The idea of braking early is to get back on the gas earlier and carry more speed through the turn. This may take a while to get used to, but riders need to remember that corner speed is often the determinant between two racers' abilities. This technique can and will often deviate depending on racing conditions. It may be necessary to go into a turn ultrahot in order to make the pass, although when the track opens up it is time to ride as efficiently as possible.

Healey stresses that racers should squeeze the bike going into braking bumps to keep it tracking straight without kicking side to side. Once you have picked a line to hit, you want to settle into the turn with as much weight as possible over the front of the bike. Getting the weight up front helps compress the fork going into the turn and keeps pressure on the front wheel for traction.

Mike Healey Motocross School student Timmy Weigand demonstrates flat corners.

Make sure to extend your leading foot in front of the bike four to six inches above the ground. Healey believes that dabbing your foot going through corners unweights the bike and can completely throw off your timing. A foot dab should only be used in emergencies.

Mike Healey takes on rutted corners.

Body position in turns is much like it is for the rest of the track: keep your arms slightly bent with your elbows up. For rutted turns you want to lean into the turns with your head over the handlebar. For flat turns it may be necessary to rotate your body to the outside of the seat and weight the outside peg. Maintaining traction throughout the turn is most important for both types.

Throttle control is another aspect of turning that Healey teaches in his schools. Being smooth with the throttle is vital; if you drop the clutch with the throttle wide-open, the rear tire is going to spin and affect forward momentum. You want to apply the power using a combination of clutch and throttle to maintain traction, in turn pulling the bike through the corner. As soon as you get off the brakes start to roll on the power to drive the bike through and out of the turn.

Under the wing of his father, Gary Bailey, David Bailey was considered one of the smoothest and most poised riders of his time. For years riders tried to copy his style. Notice his body position—practically perfect.

Once you start to exit a turn, look down the track to pick your next line. At this point you still want to maintain a consistent body position. If you let your shoulders drop back, the odds are the bike is going to oversteer; the result is the back end will want to slide out or cross-rut while exiting the turn. On the flip side, if you start to stand the bike up early, it will want to drift to the outside or jump what is left of the berm. If you keep your head and shoulders pointed toward the next section of the track, your bike will follow.

Braking is often as important as accelerating, and they both rely on traction to get the job done. The front brake is the most **BRAKING** powerful stopping tool available, although the rear brake and the engine play a role as well. Riders need to practice

SCOTT HOFFMAN

braking, like any other technique. They need to learn to feel the wheels under the bike, to find the fine line between locking up the wheels and biting the ground for stopping power. In most cases the rider is in the attack position while braking into a corner. They want to avoid locking up the rear. A skidding wheel is less effective than a spinning wheel searching for braking traction. Don't overlook engine braking as well, especially on four-strokes. Downshift to keep the rear wheel turning while slightly skidding to slow the bike. Avoid downshifting too hard; this can cause the rear to slide out and possibly stall the engine going into a turn. A good way to practice braking is to set up cones and see how deep you can brake to efficiently set up for the turn.

The mad craze among riders of all ages lately is going big, jumping that is. There is a huge difference between just hitting a jump full tilt and jumping with efficiency. Jumping can also pose the highest potential for crashing, especially over doubles and triples.

The proper jumping technique goes right back to our first tip: body position. You want to stand in a neutral position,

JUMPING that is centered on the bike with your body bent at the hip with your head slightly over the handlebar. The face of the jump and how long the face is will determine how far you need to lean into the jump. The steeper the jump face the farther a rider will have to transfer his weight forward while hitting the jump. The basic principle is that the rider is trying to stay upright while the bike rotates up the face of the jump. A good example is to take on a supercross jump. Because the jump face is so steep, racers are forced to leave the face with the handlebar almost touching their chests. If the jump face is shorter, don't stand over the handlebar as far forward; this will keep the rear end from kicking up when it leaves the ground. Flatter jumps are a lot easier to master and don't require any drastic body weight transfer.

Braking is a major part of riding that is often underestimated. As you can see, Weigand is braking hard into this right-hand corner with his body upright and his eyes looking forward picking the best line through the corner. You want to rely mostly on the front brake while applying just enough rear brake to keep the rear wheel from skidding. Also notice he keeps at least one finger on the clutch at all times.

Mike Healey likes to teach his students to brake earlier when possible; this enables a rider to get back on the gas sooner while carrying more momentum through a corner. Here, Weigand is off the brakes and set up to drive out of the flat corner. Note that left-hand turns are easier to set up for since you can drag the rear brake further into the turn because your foot remains planted on the peg longer.

Jeremy McGrath demonstrates the seat-bounce technique. He sits down on the jump face to compress the rear shock to gain added lift. This is a tricky advanced move that is usually only used for jumps with short runs or short jump faces.

BUBBA STEWART

SCOTT HOFFMAN

In addition to the standard standing position for jumps, moto jockeys have adopted a technique sometimes called the bump-seat or seat-bounce. This is when a rider leaves the face of the jump sitting down to compress the rear suspension for further lift. This practice is mostly used on smaller-faced jumps with shorter runs. This is a very tricky task and is only recommended for more experienced riders. The principle is to load the rear shock more than normal and release its force right before the rear wheel leaves the face of the jump. A pilot does this by sitting on the seat while slightly pulling back on the handlebar as the bike makes it through the transition of the jump. As the front wheel starts to leave the crest of the jump, the rider unweights the rear wheel by transferring his weight forward. This is when the spring load on the shock releases and creates more lift as the bike rises off the ground. When the bike leaves the ground, the rider is still moving forward on the bike, back into the standing attack position. If this technique is not performed correctly, it can either kick the rear wheel up and over or the bike can loop out. Be very careful when learning this technique and start off using a small bump in an open area.

Throttle control is as important when jumping as riding position. The principle rule to jumping involves leaving the face of the jump with the power on. Never chop the throttle before the bike makes it through the transition; the shock compresses and then releases prematurely and often kicks the rear wheel up causing the front end to endo. This is why we stress that you must have some forward drive up the face of a jump—that enables the bike to leave the jump face smoothly. Even if you have to brake before a jump, you should always blip the throttle going through the transition. In most cases, chop the throttle right before the rear wheel leaves the face of a jump; this will help level out the bike in the air and make for an easier landing. If you are jumping front end high, a poorly timed throttle chop may be your problem. If you consistently jump front end low, a lack of power may be the key; try holding onto the power for a split second longer.

There are many advanced principles to jumping such as tapping the rear brake in the air to drop the front end or pinning the throttle with the clutch out in the air to drop the rear wheel. These are nice to know but we recommend using them in emergency situations only. With the proper jump technique, you should not be resorting to their use on a normal basis.

Now that we have you in the air, what about landing? This depends on the landing area. If the landing area is flat, a rider should try to land slightly front end high. As the rear wheel makes contact with the ground, start to apply the power to keep the bike driving forward. On tabletop jumps and/or doubles, angle the bike in the air to match the landing area of the jump. This can be initiated when leaving the jump face or through transferring body weight forward in the air to help drop the front end slightly. On the other hand, if you are going for a large double or tabletop and you know you are going to come up short, never land front end first. This is when you should blip the throttle in the air to drop the rear wheel if necessary. Upon landing,

The clutch wasn't always used to control the power delivery. In the early days riders simply dumped the clutch at the start and pulled it in when the race was over. Kent Howerton was the first to use the clutch to control power. This early '70s shot of Howerton was the only one in a huge stack of photos from that race with a rider fingering the clutch lever. However, slipping the clutch is an often abused technique. Fanning the clutch in and out or pinning the throttle while clutching it is rarely very useful. The goal with the clutch is to feed it out or slightly slip it while applying power to search for the best combination of traction and control. Too many riders become dependent on the clutch instead of riding more efficiently. Any time the clutch is not at least partially engaged to drive the rear wheel, you may be adding precious seconds to each and every lap.

speed **secrets**

keep the power on to stiffen the rear shock. Landing with the power on can also help stop the rear end from kicking if the landing is really harsh. By no means do we advocate coming up short, but it is really nice to have a backup plan in case of an emergency.

Knowing the characteristics of a motorcycle is the first step to understanding how to ride them. The 60 to 125cc two-strokes are probably the most difficult of all bikes to control. They often lack bottom-end power and come on very strong in the middle and

CONTROLS

top-end. These bikes are full race machines and require the most clutch work to keep them pulling in the meat of their power. The smaller-bore bikes also must be revved a lot harder than larger-bore machines. Smaller-bore four-strokes are probably the easiest of all to ride; the power is very smooth and these bikes are the best tools for beginning riders.

The 250cc two-strokes are the staple ride of most motocrossers. The bikes don't require as much clutch work as a 125 and they are better suited for riders over 160 pounds. Except for the new YZ250F four-stroke, most 250cc four-strokes are fairly tame trailbikes that are very easy to ride. However, the YZ250F is a full-blown motocross bike that is slated to race against 125 two-strokes. This bike is very high-strung and likes to be revved to the moon and ridden like a 125.

Four-strokes pretty much own the big-bore class today, that is except for a few fleeting two-strokes from Honda, Kawasaki and KTM. The big-bore four-strokes produce a lot of torquey power that is easy to ride but can be a handful for the inexperienced rider.

In order to become a better rider you need to have a bike that is set up for you, with the right bar bend, lever position and seat height on top of the basic suspension settings. A lot of this is based on personal preference, although if the setup is off drastically, it can affect your ability to improve as a rider. Consult your owner's manual or talk to a race shop or local riding instructor for help.

Just because you have the riding style of Travis Pastrana doesn't mean you are in the black. An ill-prepared bike can throw off even the best rider's skills. If you are not schooled in this field, we suggest first reading the owner's or service manual you tossed to the side when you bought the bike. If you bought your ride used, go to the dealer and buy one. Most manuals offer detailed information on basic bike setup.

The first step to setting up a bike is to adjust the bar position and lever arrangement. You want to run a handlebar that is not swept back too far. Position the bar in the clamp so the end of the bar is not higher than the leading line of the grip. Tall riders may find that a taller bar or clamps may fit their body position more efficiently.

With the controls in place, it is time to check the basic suspension settings. Setting the race sag is the most important. This needs to be done with the rider fully dressed in riding gear. Race sag is the difference between the rear axle and the seat when the bike is on the

BIKE SETUP

stand and when the rider is sitting on the bike. The difference should be between 95 and 100mm for 125cc bikes on up. The 80cc bikes should fall in the range between 90 and 95mm. After race sag is set, check the free sag; this is done by sitting the bike on the ground under its own weight. Lift up on the rear fender, you should have between one and two inches of free sag. If the shock has one inch

10 MOST COMMON MISTAKES

- Not practicing. Practice means practice.
- Going fast instead of going smart.
- Not knowing your limits.
- Riders often don't look far enough ahead.
- Forgetting the clutch. Keep a finger on the clutch at all times.
- Riding stiff. Try to stay loose and don't fight the bike, it will always win.
- Not enough racers practice starts. This is the only time a rider has the potential to pass 39 riders in one shot.
- Don't follow a rider too closely; pick alternative lines when possible.
- Line choice—riders tend to stick to the main line that is the roughest and most rutted-out one on the track. Seek out smoother and faster lines.
- Abusing the clutch—too many riders just pin the throttle while fanning the clutch to death. Feed the clutch out while twisting the throttle for best results.

or less, odds are you will need a stiffer shock spring.

These are basic settings, if the bike was bought used, it is a good idea to set the clickers on the shock and fork back to the standard clicker settings stated in the owner's manual. For further suspension tuning you should consult your local dealer or suspension tuner.

60cc	80cc	125cc	250cc	Open

Virtually every riding tip in this special section has a viable application for off-road. Just about any obstacle that can be built on a motocross course appears somewhere—perhaps in lessened scale—in a natural trail setting. Plus, many trails traverse areas that have been mined, logged or quar-

SPECIAL OFF-ROAD SECTION

ried, and they have sections that are literally man-made. One caveat: while any tip that applies to motocross applies to off-road, the reverse may not be true. These tips are specific to off-road, and they can make the difference between pleasure and pain on the trail.

speed secrets

TWINKLE TOES: Ride with the balls of your feet on the footpegs. Motocrossers still use this tip in deep ruts, but with the high-impact landings of current tracks, this is more of an off-road technique these days. The tip demands that you ride light on your feet and keep your feet moving, since you need to reposition to brake or shift. This is Kawasaki GNCC star Fred Andrews demonstrating how he protects his toes from rocks and stumps while standing. He has the ball of his foot over the peg and his toes pointed up a bit as well. If you do kick a hidden object, your foot will get knocked off the peg but hopefully without smashing anything tender. Andrews also keeps his boot toes tucked up next to the engine. That does provide some additional protection for the feet and toes, but this foot position is mainly to protect knees from injury. If you catch your toe and it gets pulled back, your knee or ankle can truly suffer.

PUSH ON, NOT UP: Every rider, no matter how good they are, ends up paddling or pushing. There is a definite method to push while riding. If you are already in a have-to-push situation, your bike needs all the traction it can get to maintain forward motion. You need to keep as much of your weight as possible dead in the saddle to help the rear tire bite. Push with your feet, but push forward. Do not push your weight up off the seat. Also, try to keep the rear wheel from spinning. Work the throttle and clutch with your rear wheel weighted to prevent wheelspin. If the bike stops and starts spinning, cut power immediately before you dig a hole and let the bike roll back a bit. Then try to go forward with a little momentum and get past the place you got stuck before.

EYES UP: The farther you look down the trail, the faster (and safer) you will be able to ride. Target fixation is another reason this tip is important. You will go where you are looking, so look where you want to go, not where you are afraid you might go. Notice in this photo of Team Green's Andrews that he is looking well down the trail despite bowing almost to the tank to clear this log. If your front fender falls off, you shouldn't notice. Don't be looking right in front of your bike's wheel.

FOOLS RUSH IN: This is Andrews in an actual race. He obviously isn't in a hurry to charge this mud hole. Our photos of the novice riders show big wheelies, big splashes and big crashes. Taking a moment to check out the situation is time saved, not time wasted. This advice applies to any obstacle, not just mud or water.

PAPA WHEELIE: Wheelies aren't just to show off. There are many situations off-road where the key to keeping the front wheel from being bounced or ripped out of line is to keep it from hitting the obstacle in the first place. Many times a well-timed, short, low wheelie will allow the front wheel to float over sharp or angled rocks, slippery roots, holes and ditches or even small steps or ledges. Also, there are instances when it is easier to keep the bike on the ground and driving if you loft the front wheel over a bump and let the rear wheel soak it up. A wheelie is an absolutely vital part of any off-road repertoire.

DOUBLE DOWN: This is the riding position for downhills—even steep and scary ones. Don't go down hills sitting down. That further weights the front end, fatigues your arms, prevents the suspension from working correctly and makes you look like a beginner. Standing in this position allows the bike's suspension to work properly and your knees, elbows and hips to act as body suspension. No matter what you do, the front wheel will have all the weight it can stand. Your job is to keep weight on the rear wheel and maintain directional control. It is always better to go faster than you feel comfortable than it is to lock up the wheels and lose steering control.

EDITORS' top tips

speed secrets

SCOTT HOFFMAN

- I believe that knowing one's limits is one of the most important parts of becoming a better rider. At that point riders can gradually push themselves to the next level.
- The clutch and throttle are some of the most abused parts by both motocross and off-road riders. Grabbing a handful of throttle while fanning the clutch to death to control one's speed is one of the most common mistakes I have seen at the track. Riders need to learn to feed the throttle to control the power to the ground while slightly slipping the clutch.
- Slow down before you learn to go fast. One day back in '87 I passed local pro Rich Truchinski in practice, but I was all over the track on the verge of crashing any second. He told me that if I just slowed down I would start winning races. That week I removed the "Win or Bail" goon sticker from the back of my pants and started to put my riding style on sedatives. Before I knew it I was collecting trophies instead of hospital receipts.

- Line selection. Picking lines is an art and many riders never pay enough attention to finding smoother lines, especially when a track becomes littered with square-edged holes and nasty braking and acceleration bumps. Learn to spot smoother lines during a race; they save energy and can open the doors to alternate passing lanes.

KEN FAUGHT

- During motocross starts, one of the things that I learned a few years ago was to load the front suspension. Just before the gate drops, I grab onto the front brake and let the clutch out just enough to keep tension on the fork springs. With the fork slightly compressed, the bike tends to wheelie less, plus the lag time of the clutch is reduced since it's already slightly grabbing.

- One of the best hillclimbing tips I ever received was from Larry Roeseler. He pointed out that you should strive to keep both feet on the footpegs while leaning forward. Your feet allow you to grip the bike and keep from sliding toward the back of the seat. When your legs start to flail and your body slides, your bike will want to wheelie more, plus you lose most of your side-to-side control.
- On downhills, one of the most important things I ever learned was to drag the rear brake a little to settle the suspension, even when accelerating. This also helps eliminate headshake because the back end can't come around on you as easily.
- When we were kids, Jeremy McGrath showed me to use the front brake to settle the front wheel into ruts. This keeps the front end from wanting to ride up on the outside lip and jump out of the line. This technique takes a little while to get used to.
- When riding in thick mud, Scott Summers taught me the importance of keeping the tires clean. He usually looks for a patch of grass or something abrasive enough to pull the mud off the tires. If that doesn't work, he upshifts one gear taller than normal race/trail pace, grabs the clutch, pins the throttle and then releases the clutch. This intentional wheelspin will fling the mud off in a matter of seconds. To do this correctly, you should be going in a straight line, and you may have to do this often.

BRYAN NYLANDER

- Relax, let the bike float over trail obstacles. When you fight the front end over sections the bike has a tendency to throw off a rider's balance.
- Ride smoothly. It didn't take long for me to realize that a motorcycle is stronger than I am. If you ride smooth and try to flow from turn to turn or obstacle, you will conserve a great deal of energy, especially on long rides or races.

- On hills, control the power with the clutch. When climbing hills there is a fine line between too much and too little traction, this is where clutch control is key. If a rider chops the throttle, even for a split second, forward momentum is lost. With the clutch, a rider can maintain a consistent throttle while still controlling the power delivery to the ground. If the wheel starts to hook up too much, just slip the clutch slightly. If the bike starts to bog but it's not enough to require downshifting, slip the clutch to get the engine back into the meat of the power curve.
- Keep your butt on the seat to keep the rear wheel planted. This is a great trick when riding in slippery or wet conditions. When riders get stuck in ruts, they lift their feet off the pegs and try to push the bike with their feet. As soon as you unweight the rear end, the rear tire loses its traction and just spins. It is best to keep your body weight planted on the seat while you try to lug the bike up the hill. Don't just pin the throttle and dump the clutch; try to finesse the bike up a hill using throttle and clutch control.
- Look ahead, so you can choose lines and anticipate trail obstacles.

KAREL KRAMER

- I once shot photos of eight-time national enduro champ Dick Burleson teaching a beginner riding school. I wasn't there to learn anything, I was just the photographer, but I came away with two tips that made huge improvements in my speed and confidence for motocross and off-road. I figured I was pretty good at motocross, and my technique was to stand up, get my weight back and lock my arms straight for severe drops. Burleson told his students they needed to keep a little bend in their elbows at all times. He explained that even a small drop-off or unseen impact to the front wheel would completely jerk the rider out of position and possibly over the handlebar when his/her elbows were locked. A light went on: So that's why that happens! Learning to keep that little bend in my elbows to handle unseen jolts helped my speed and confidence on downhills more than any tip I've ever learned.
- I learned a second great moto tip from enduro ace Burleson. One pretty successful female off-road rider he was teaching had been a local champ, but DB stilled critiqued her entire riding position. She rode standing most of the time, and DB gave her kudos for that, but explained that she rode standing very straight. He explained the advantages of "getting small." At her height (or his) there seemed little reason to be in a racer's crouch. He explained she'd have better control if she kept her weight compact over the bike. Look at pictures of Scott Summers. He is a tall rider, but even when standing he has almost a 90-degree bend to his knees, a significant bend at the hips and at the shoulders and elbows. I liken it to the stance wrestlers assume at the start of a match. They are poised to move in any direction, yet aren't burning energy. As a tall rider I found the advice he gave the local champ to be even more effective. When I really want to bump up my aggression on the track or trail, I get small.
- I used to race night motocross at Ascot Park. The track was largely flat, hard, slick clay. I was never totally comfortable in the flat turns. I also trail ride with ex-dirt tracker John Hateley. Hateley was an Ascot legend on a Triumph, and I made an off-hand comment to the effect that I couldn't fathom how he could turn so fast on the flat clay. I told him I was slip-sliding the front wheel around the TT turn every lap. He shrugged and said, "You probably shut the throttle." A motorcycle is made to turn with the throttle on, and even a tiny throttle opening will allow the front wheel to stay planted. Now I try never to chop the throttle suddenly, or shut it off all the way in a turn, because he was right. When I concentrate on accelerating just a tiny bit through turns, the front wheel stays planted.

Trails

CHAPTER FIVE

Kevin Hines: Bounding through boulder fields 105
Guy Cooper: How to avoid hang-ups on logs 106
Kevin Hines on single-track off-camber trails 107
Scott Summers' riding tip handbook .108
Dick Burleson on crossing big, angled logs 111
Kevin Hines with slalom speed secrets for woods racers 112
Dick Burleson on small-log crossings 113
Randy Hawkins on uphill switchbacks 114
Lafferty takes on drop-offs 115
Mastering mud ditches 116
Johnny Campbell attacks high-speed G-outs 117
Thinking wet 118
Riding high-speed fire roads with Johnny Campbell 119

1 "Focusing ahead, of course, is real important," Hines stresses. "I'm coming down the straightaway and starting to make my corner, and I can see where I want to be. If I were to try to avoid all the rocks and go wide, I would lose seconds—seconds in every corner add up to minutes. I'm braking a little bit coming into the corner."

2 "I tend not to notice the size of the rocks [when looking for a takeoff point]," Hines reveals. "I go the straightest line I possibly can at all times. I like to stay on top of the rocks if I can, because if you get off to the edge of them, you could bend your disc or your sprocket, or break off a footpeg. So I tend to go over the center of rocks as much as I can. A lot of people don't do that, but it's definitely the shortest line. I clutch it on the face of the rock—very smooth, just a little bit of clutch, a little jump. Just lighten up when you hit the rock face and jump over it."

3 A side view shows how Hines hits the take-off rock squarely in the center. He's standing with some bend in his knees, not only to help absorb impact shock but also to get lift after hitting the rock by straightening them out.

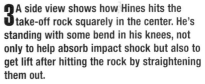

4 A bit of clutch, smoothly done, helps get more lift as well. Notice that Hines is straightening his legs now that the bike's taking off and that he remains centered while the bike moves beneath him.

5 All that's left is to hang on and enjoy the ride! Before he lands, Hines will pull himself farther forward, which simultaneously lightens the rear and forces the front down: He doesn't want the rear tire to land on the short side of the rocks that his front end's passing over now.

105

GUY COOPER
HOW TO HANDLE
HANG-UPS ON LOGS

There will be times in every dirt rider's career that he won't be able to get over a log cleanly. Instead of bouncing over gracefully like a trials rider, the bike will get hung up for any number of reasons. When that happens, what should you do? We asked Suzuki's Guy Cooper to demonstrate.

As a trials rider, he emphasizes throttle control when the rear tire comes into contact with the log: "If you hold the throttle open, you'll [get too much] wheelspin, you won't get traction, and the bike will spit out sideways," he cautions. Also guard against excessive speed, as that may toss you onto your head.

1 "When I first approach this log, I see that the height is questionable and that there is a possibility that I might endo over the back side. My speed is just fast enough to slide the skid plate over the log [after wheeling on the approach]. My legs are extended so that, as the bike hits the log, they act as dampers to the jolt and can also help the bike's movement over the log."

2 "My [approach] speed was cautious and maybe a little too slow. I had to think fast and catch the log with my feet. [I'm about to] transfer my weight way over the front to get my RMX to teeter-totter, if you will."

3 "I'm preparing to push off. Making it to this point is fairly easy at low speeds. Use caution here. Too much speed sets you up for the classic 'flying W.' The push-off is the most important part. Generally, it's not the frame rails or linkage that hold you up—it's the rear wheel. Unfortunately for us short guys, our legs aren't long enough to push on the log once the bike gets hung up. At this point, the push-off determines whether there's enough momentum to bring the rear wheel over the log. As the wheel…comes into contact with the log, I need to help [the rear tire gain traction]. This is done by putting my feet back onto the pegs, which [weights] the bike, allowing the suspension to absorb some of the log's height. Leave your legs behind on the log, and [the amount] your butt [gets kicked by the seat will be] in direct [proportion] to the log size and [your] speed. Too much of either, and…your boot soles see sunshine!"

PHOTOS: KEN FAUGHT

KEVIN HINES ON SINGLE-TRACK OFF-CAMBER TRAILS

A lot separates a good trail rider from a great one and technical sections such as single-track off-camber trails certainly illustrate the difference. We asked seasoned off-road expert Kevin Hines to demonstrate how skill, accuracy, body position and safety all come into play when negotiating sections like those on our 24-hour test track.

1 "The most important aspect of riding off-camber single-tracks is body position. The rider should be standing and weighting the outside peg for optimum traction. It's best to keep your body over the bike without leaning too much, as this will keep the bike tracking straight on the trail. It's also important to keep your eyes focused in front of the bike and not down at the front wheel. A lot of riders make this mistake and often over-correct. This could easily send you off a narrow single-track trail. It's best to use body English to achieve balance. Because the trail is often only slightly wider than a tire, steering your way out of a mistake is not an option. You need to change your body position to correct the bike. Again, weighting the outside peg is key for proper traction. Try to keep your body over the center of the bike. If your weight is too far back, there won't be enough bite on the front wheel and you may lose control."

2 "Smooth power delivery is the key to keeping momentum through technical sections. If you gas it too hard, the rear wheel could spin and slip off the trail, or it could lift the front wheel and cause a loss of steering control. If there's a section you need to climb, keep up as much momentum as possible and use the torque for maximum traction. A word to the wise: Practice this technique on easy trails before tackling difficult cliff-hangers."

1 The bike had to be shipped to Finland early. It is basically complete, but will have the race suspension and other special parts installed shortly before the event.

2 The engine is totally stock with stock displacement, although a Wiseco piston goes in as soon as Fred Bramblett, Summers's mechanic, uncrates the bike. Carburetion is stock as well. The Twin Air air filter and Yoshimura exhaust system constitute the only mods.

3 Summers relies exclusively on Tsubaki O-ring chains, and both Bramblett and Summers report zero failures in all their years racing with them.

4 At his last ISDE, Summers had wheel trouble in a motocross special test, so White Brothers suggested that he start Finland with these special gold-anodized wheels built with Talon billet hubs, Takasago Excel rims and heavy-duty spokes.

5 A handmade, works two-piece clutch cover like he uses in the U.S. is installed in case the clutch needs replacing on the trail or during the event.

6 He'll run the same Pirelli Lagunacross front tire he normally uses at all U.S. races but with a Michelin Bib Mousse installed.

7 Pirelli's FIM–approved MT18 tire is installed on the rear. It looks like an aggressive sand/mud tire but has shorter knobs. It gets a Mousse as well. In the U.S., Summers runs a Garacross rear tire almost exclusively.

8 Summers prefers the stock seat foam and cover, but only uses a seat for two races before it is relegated to just practice duty. The ISDE bike hit the crate with a brand-new one.

9 The plastic looks perfectly stock, but, in fact, UFO in Italy manufactures all but the tank. We watched as the sidepanels were installed. They fit perfectly.

Inside Scott Summers's

10 The handlebar is a Summers–bend Answer ProTaper, cut to 29.5 inches. Although a replica of the stock XR bend, the ProTaper has some flex that makes it easier on the hands throughout a long race.

11 Two throttle tubes, cut and spliced together, afford more thumb clearance from the throttle housing until a billet unit is

made. The return cable is removed, its mount cut from the throttle housing and a small plate heliarced over the hole.

12 Summers Racing Components is developing these special aluminum hand guards. The inboard mount attaches to the top triple clamp. This provides more cable and hose room than a standard bar-mounted setup, but the inboard end is not solidly mounted. It can rotate on the bolt enough to allow the handlebar to flex, while a standard aluminum hand guard would take the flex out of the bar.

13 Summers claims that the trick Yoshimura tapered stainless steel headpipes and muffler are

the single biggest power improvement he has developed for the motor.

14 The two-piece clutch cover looks quite exotic and substantially decreases clutch replacement time. It's no longer used for Nationals, however. The competition is so close that changing a clutch would put any rider out of the points for the day. Bramblett keeps fresh clutches in the bikes, and Summers keeps them alive or DNFs.

15 On the front of the engine is a Summers Racing Components (SRC) guard to keep the pulse-generator wire and grommet from ripping out. When the engine is extremely hot, the grommet becomes soft; if it comes out, the engine loses the oil.

1996 ISDE XR600R

21 The most visible of the SRC products is this light and strong fork brace. It provides the rigidity and steering precision of an inverted fork design, yet allows use of the excellent stock fork. Summers runs stock valving in the fork with '87 Honda CR500R springs and an oil level of 120 millimeters.

22 Yoshimura built this special exhaust system for the ISDE. It sound tests at 93 dbA, is mounted solidly to last six full days of torture and lost only one horsepower in the midrange over the open race system. It actually makes more power on top.The pipe end turns in toward the bike, rather than down, as does the production part.

23 Normally, the taillight lens is installed for looks only, but Bramblett wired it up on the ISDE bike.

24 In the past, Summers had Bramblett install an oil cooler from Honda's XR250R, but the new XR400R has a larger oil cooler, so he uses that unit now.

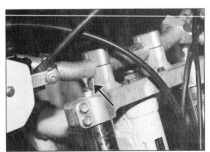

25 Many of the mods to Summers's XR *add* weight, so trimming the fat in other areas became crucial. Losing the large bolts that normally hold the ProTaper mounts to the top triple clamp by welding the mounts on helped a little.

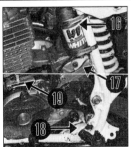

16 This WP shock is so old that the red anodizing on the reservoir has faded, but Summers has never found one that works better. Even exact copies feel different on the trail and graph differently on the shock dyno. He guards this favored shock like pure gold!

17 SRC calls this front chain guide/case protector a "Kiwi," since it looks like a bird's head.

18 Both footpeg mounts are gusseted and strengthened, and extra-strong IMS footpegs are used.

19 Since SRC extends the clutch arm, it installs a clutch-cable retainer to relocate the cable mount for it, too. The process greatly eases clutch-pull effort and bulletproofs the cable mounting.

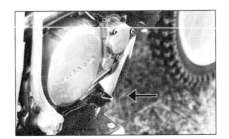

20 SRC is developing this new aluminum engine guard bar. It's a modification of the stock unit that has this little aluminum "fairing" or wedge-shaped affair in front of the brake pedal and the shifter. Filled with rubber, it nearly rests against the engine cases. This allows the rider to plow through rocks and stumps without damaging the controls.

PHOTOS: KAREL KRAMER

FLY INSTEAD OF SPLASH

Several types of off-road events allow no preriding but do allow riders to walk or bicycle the course before a race. Top-level competitors aren't content to merely see where the course goes, however; they want to plot legal lines that will save time or allow them to pass. Summers showed us this example on his practice track. The normal line requires an off-camber turn in a muddy, rocky bank. Just one foot off to the side of the most common trail is a rock on the edge of the creek bank. Seeing that rock proved to be a major advantage for Summers.

1 "There is a rock solidly embedded near the edge of a steep creek bank, and it is sticking up enough to get my bike's suspension to work a bit. This is the perfect example of a line I look for—I hope I'm the only one who sees it!

"It is difficult to maintain momentum through the woods on the approach to the rock. I have to be sure of my balance, since there is only about one bike-length to accelerate when I finally approach the rock. I'm standing by now, and in that last bike-length, I push down on the suspension with my legs to load it into the rock. I rev the bike, then slip the clutch as hard as traction will allow right as the front wheel hits the rock."

2 "As the forward motion of the acceleration and the rebound of the suspension lofts the bike into the air, I let the bike come up toward me to aid the lift while pushing down and away on the bar. I want a front-wheel landing here. It will be softer and require less energy, plus I want to ensure that the rear wheel stays in the air as long as possible so that it can clear the opposite bank, if possible."

3 "I land with my weight recentered and in my attack position. I grip the bike with my knees and accelerate hard as I land, so that I can transform the impact into traction. I'm always looking for those spots that the rear wheel can hook up in to increase the bike's speed and control."

4 "This is what I'm hoping the competition is doing: slowing down for the off-camber and preparing to change directions. They'll be losing speed right where I pick it up."

5 "How fast does this look? I'm tip-toeing through slippery rocks, concentrating on not losing the front end instead of flying past this whole mess and getting back on the gas. Alternate lines are definitely worth looking for! They can make the difference between winning and losing, besides making events more fun, and easier on you and the bike. That's a win-win situation!"

PHOTOS: KAREL KRAMER

DICK BURLESON ON CROSSING BIG, ANGLED LOGS

You don't often find big logs lying at an angle in the trail because most dirt riders will either approach angled logs from a more perpendicular angle or avoid them entirely. Plus, only more advanced riders would consider such obstacles.

However, you may find yourself faced with such a challenge in order to save time and distance—or maybe pass your buddy or a competitor. We asked eight-time AMA National Enduro Champion Dick Burleson how he'd advise someone to overcome the dreaded huge fallen tree at an angle. "The key thing is to let [the bike] work underneath you, sort of like you're a downhill skier," he analyzes.

1 "As I approach the log, I see that there are two paths: the conventional one, which is pretty far out of the way (I'd have to really slow down) and the one going over the log—a good place to possibly pass," Burleson says. "The only *real* reason to do this is a passing situation. It's a pretty big log, so I know I can't hit it with big speed or I'll just go over the bar. I'm down in first gear, just feathering the throttle, and [I want to be] completely up on the pegs. As I get about five or six feet away from the tree, I give it some throttle so that the front tire lifts—I want to clear this thing completely because it's such an extreme angle. I want the front tire to clear the log totally, so I have no deflection in the front."

2 "[I use] enough throttle to get the front wheel up and all the way over, but not so much that I go for the sky. If you get the front end too high, then you get too much reaction in the rear. Once the front end's completely over the log, I get my weight back a little bit—not way, way, *way* back. The front tire goes over, and immediately I ease up on the throttle. You don't want to close the throttle [all the way instantly], because what helps the [rear] tire go over [the log] at such an angle is if it's spinning evenly, more or less without the brakes or acceleration. If the [rear] tire's trying to get traction with either brakes or acceleration, it'll want to [slide] along the [top of] the log."

3 "I just roll the throttle back so that it's almost like it went into neutral; I've got my hand on the clutch, too. Then I transfer my weight forward to allow the back of the bike to work and go over the log. That's more or less one of the keys to it: The back of the bike has to be free to come up over the log. If you've got your weight too far back, the back end won't be able to come [up]. It'll just stuff [into the log]. And if you're way too far forward, you might get knocked over the bar. There's a middle ground there."

4 "In order to keep the tire from going completely sideways, you've got to keep the bike gripped tightly between your knees. Your feet are still on the pegs. Let the back of the bike move around underneath you; it's gonna probably slide off to the side because of the angle of the log, but that's okay. What's important is the position of your upper body—from your hips up to your head. Where's that going? Let the back of the bike slide, and your legs and knees work underneath you, sort of like a downhill skier. That's the important thing: that the front of the bike is going straight because you got it completely over [the log], and then the back of the bike works just a little bit, and you let it go underneath you to the side."

5 This (or worse) is what can happen if you get a little too throttle-happy or chop the throttle when the rear tire gets on top of the log. You want neutral throttle, coupled with a forward weight shift. The bike will probably go a little sideways; let it do so by keeping your lower body supple and reactive like a slalom skier's.

PHOTOS: MARK KARIYA

111

KEVIN HINES WITH SLALOM SPEED SECRETS FOR WOODS RACERS

Most dirt riders like trails where they can keep some speed and momentum; it's just more fun. And when the trail snakes through fairly tightly spaced trees, being able to thread your way through quickly without hitting any of them heavily guarantees you're going to have a better time than the poor sap who ends up mimicking a pinball.

As a former AMA National Enduro Champion (and still a top woods racer), Kevin Hines knows it takes more than narrow handlebars to slalom through trees. Here's his advice.

1 "I'm coming into [this section] at a pretty high rate of speed," Hines observes, "and I'm using the front brake heavily to keep the front end down. It's a lot easier to steer if the front end's lower. I have my head way over the front of the motorcycle when I'm doing it, trying to get all my weight forward to make the front end very precise and as low as possible."

2 "I'm trying to keep the throttle as steady as I possibly can and use the clutch, feathering it all the way through to get perfect traction and drive."

3 Hines does not suggest tossing the bike from side to side through trees. "I have to move [the bike] a little bit," he admits, "but I'd rather graze a tree [with my hand guard] than overexaggerate and waste time swinging the bike from side to side."

4 "Steering with my feet is the big thing. I'm on the balls of my feet, and I'm manipulating the bike side to side, rocking with my feet, not with my arms. I'm trying to keep my upper body in pretty much a fixed position and use my feet to steer. My knees are always against the tank of the motorcycle, and that helps.

PHOTOS: MARK KARIYA

DICK BURLESON ON SMALL-LOG CROSSINGS

If you ride in the woods, you're going to find small trees that have fallen in your path. They're simply one of the obstacles that make woods riding and racing interesting and fun.

Of course, knowing exactly *how* to tackle them enhances one's enjoyment, as well. Not knowing how tends to make such trail challenges an annoyance that robs you of momentum. We asked eight-time AMA National enduro champ Dick Burleson to explain how he approaches small logs in the trail.

1 Here, Burleson has completed a turn in the trail and is now heading down a straight section, complicated by the fallen sapling and a jog near the end. "When I look up the trail, I see the small log," he begins. "Also, I'm looking *past* the log to my landing zone, and there are a couple little trees on the outside with a left-hand turn. The log has been beaten down a lot because of guys going over it, so it's low enough that I don't have to wheelie the front wheel, then get the back wheel over it. I can carry good speed. With this one, you hit it like a jump."

2 "You've got to get off the seat. As I approach, I line up—try to get as square as I can to the log so that the bike doesn't want to kick too much one way or the other. [Here], I'm fully up off the seat, and I have pretty good control of the bike by using the pegs and squeezing [the seat] with my knees to keep the bike going straight in case it wants to kick a little bit. I'm keeping my upper body pretty low. Just as I hit it, I get my weight back a little bit to let the front wheel come up. I try to absorb the impact as best as I can with my legs."

PHOTOS: MARK KARIYA

3 "I've got a finger on the clutch and a finger on the brake so that when I land I can immediately make the turn. I'm looking up the trail to see where it goes. You can't just look at it, then bring your field of vision in really close. Keep looking down the trail so you [don't] crash into the trees on the other end."

RANDY HAWKINS ON UPHILL SWITCHBACKS

Riding on tight trails is hard enough, but when you throw in elements like uphill switchbacks things can get nasty. Some combinations of riding techniques enable a rider to slice his way through even the gnarliest sections. Randy Hawkins and his new Yamaha YZ400F show us the easiest way to tackle these kinds of sections.

1 "Because the trail is extremely tight I have to use the existing rut to take on the section. Let the bike settle into the rut and allow the rut to guide you around the corner. On switchbacks like this one the rut will guide you directly into the next turn. Braking is also important when riding ruts. I like to brake early so I can accelerate through the rut. I try to complete my braking before I enter the turn."

2 "As I come out of the first turn I'm looking forward to set up for the next one. I try not to gas it too hard out of the corner when going from turn to turn. You need to be smooth. Get a good drive out of the first corner and you can keep the power delivery smooth to the next turn."

3 "As you can see, I'm following the rut around, completely changing my direction. Because I exited the first turn smoothly I have no trouble keeping up momentum and have started a rhythm from turn to turn. Again, because I've maintained smooth throttle control and neutral body position I'm able to keep the wheels in the rut. If I were on the power too hard, the front wheel would likely jump or ride out of the rut and throw off my rhythm. Riding too aggressively in technical sections can actually cause you to lose time. It's best to slow down and ride smooth. You'll be surprised how fast you go."

114

PHOTOS: SCOTT HOFFMAN

LAFFERTY TAKES ON DROP-OFFS

If you ride off off-road, you will encounter drop-offs in some form. There are only two ways to attack these sections—really slow or really fast—there is no in-between. If you're not sure what's on the other side of the drop-off or you're not sure you can clear it, it's best to ride slow and roll down the obstacle if possible. On the other hand, some drop-offs have ditches or are too steep to roll down. In these cases, jumping is the only solution. Here, '97 national enduro champion Mike Lafferty shows us the proper way to jump drop-offs.

1 "One of the first things to remember when you have committed to jumping a drop-off is to carry your momentum off the jump. As you can see from the first photo, I'm in a stable riding position with my weight centered on the bike. As I approach the jump I'm looking forward to locate the landing area. If the landing area has ruts or rocks, pick the best line possible. As I approach the jump, I keep my body weight low so when I reach the face of the drop-off, I can load the rear suspension and gas it to bring the front end up or at least keep it from dropping down."

2 "Right before I leave the face of the jump I apply some power and at the same time I start to move my weight slightly back and stand up—this helps keep the bike level, slightly elevating the front wheel as the bike leaves the face of the ledge. Here the front wheel is just starting to leave the drop-off and I always try to keep the front wheel from dropping down. It's important to keep up momentum in order to clear holes or kickers on the landing. Even if there is a turn after the drop-off, try to clear the obstacles or at least get the front wheel over them."

3 "Here I have successfully made the drop-off and I'm starting to make the landing. I land with the rear wheel first, but I've moved my weight forward to balance out the bike on the landing. I am still looking forward for possible obstacles in the trail. In this case, there is no immediate turn after the drop-off so I start to get back on the gas as soon as the rear wheel makes contact with the ground. There are several types of drop-offs and I don't suggest inexperienced riders start jumping 10-foot drop-offs. Instead, use this technique to start on small obstacles and work your way up."

pro riding PRS secrets

MASTERING MUD DITCHES

Muddy ditches are common off-road obstacles, but that doesn't make them any more fun. You need to get through them as quickly as possible without falling, bogging your bike or splashing muck on yourself. Muddy gloves and grips can put you in reverse faster than you can imagine.

One of our editors raced the morning race at the Okeechobee GNCC opener, and he was curious how the heroes handled this stinky black mudhole. He'd ridden well to the side, taking a lot of time to miss the deepest ruts and much of the slick, shiny black slime. He was pretty stunned when Ty Davis and Fred Andrews never let off the gas!

The key to their strategy is twofold: Maintain speed and try to jump as far over the mud ditch as possible while radically exaggerating the front end lift to keep the goo off and get the front tire as far toward dry dirt as possible.

Scott Summers runs soft suspension and his bike is heavy, so he aimed for a spot that kept the rear wheel on the ground all the way. But note the radical wheelie angle he has chosen. The mud will slow the bike dramatically, so there is little danger of looping out if his timing is right. He also gets the front wheel as far across the obstacle as possible.

Guy Cooper chose a spot that required him to jump into the ditch. However, he still maintains a fairly radical front wheel elevation into the mud. By choosing this tack, Cooper, like Summers, also keeps his bike's front wheel and boots from plowing into the goo, thereby blowing slime up onto the handlebar.

Fred Andrews uses the same technique. Notice he isn't hanging off the back of the bike. When the rear wheel hits the bank, the rear end *will* kick up. Andrews keeps his weight centered, allowing him to use leg action to absorb the hit. He also keeps his body in the middle of the bike, so if it kicks to the side, it can pivot a little without tossing his weight to one side.

Even though Ty Davis was one of the first riders to wheelie the ditch, he was not committed to this method. If there was traffic that kept him from hitting the ditch where the ruts were shallow, he stayed safe, slowed way down and still attempted to keep those gloves, goggles and grips slime-free. After all, it is a *long* race.

pro riding secrets

PHOTOS: MATT FREEMAN

"In desert racing, speeds are high and concentration is of the utmost importance. If I'm riding in dust, I have to react and make decisions very quickly. As I approach this particular G-out I'm in attack position and scanning for the less severe line. After I've chosen my line, I lightly back off the throttle and look ahead to see the other side. This G-out is too deep to wheelie into and too long to jump across, so I'll have to jump into it. This particular G-out has a dip before it so I chop the throttle and use the dip as a jump into the G-out. Be careful not to carry too much speed—you can slam into the other side and endo. I'm toward the rear of the bike and I'm keeping the front end light to help absorb the landing."

"The landing is hard, but because of my neutral body position I am able to absorb some of the impact. As I land at the bottom, I change my body position and focus on the terrain ahead. I'm also paying close attention to getting on the throttle and rebounding out of the G-out, clearing as many obstacles on the other side as possible. By slipping the clutch and unweighting the motorcycle, I'm preparing to loft over the next obstacle—in this case, a series of whoops."

JOHNNY CAMPBELL ATTACKS HIGH-SPEED G-OUTS

One of the most dangerous obstacles in high-speed desert racing is the G-out. When you're riding at a blistering pace, these land blemishes are difficult to see, especially in the dust. Whether the G-out is steep and deep or gradual, it can throw you over the bar if you're not careful.

Identifying the obstacle and setting up for impact is critical. On his big XR600R, Baja champ Johnny Campbell demonstrates the safest and quickest way to attack a G-out without damaging any bike or body parts.

By Matt Freeman

"I jump out of the G-out and clear some rocky terrain in the process. Because I didn't slam into the G-out with my front wheel first I saved some time and energy and didn't put my bike at risk. Right after leaping out of the G-out I'm back in attack position and ready to land the bike and move onto the next obstacle."

117

pro riding secrets

THINKING WET

At most of the recent GNCC events we have attended, there has been at least one good deep-water crossing somewhere on the course. Naturally, we gathered our cameras and headed out to the Grand Nationals in hopes of snagging some great photos of the leaders blasting through the water. In every case we were disappointed. Not one of the front-runners splashed around. They know that a long race with wet gear, dripping goggles and doused gloves is no fun. The goggles and gloves can be a genuine safety hazard and at the very least will make it difficult to see and hang on. The top riders eased into the water, rode through slowly and stayed as dry as possible. This is just one more case where it pays to emulate the heroes.

While waiting for the leaders, we saw plenty of lappers blasting through the water of this shallow stream. This kind of recklessness can make you miserable, uncomfortable and possibly jeopardize your safety—and that's if you don't hit any hidden holes or rocks under the water!

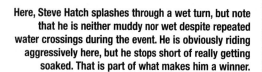

Here, Steve Hatch splashes through a wet turn, but note that he is neither muddy nor wet despite repeated water crossings during the event. He is obviously riding aggressively here, but he stops short of really getting soaked. That is part of what makes him a winner.

Former World Enduro Champ Paul Edmondson is famous as a mud and wet-weather rider. Here, he not only creeps through this water crossing at the Boyers GNCC, he attempts to lift his boots out of the water and keeps the splashing down to avoid soaking his gloves and goggles. Before entering the stream he came to a near stop, judged the situation and made a line choice before continuing. He even waited until other riders were clear of the liquid before entering the stream. The time he spends here will pay off when he can ride more aggressively for the remainder of the race.

[FACT] Yamaha-mounted Tom Webb won the Desert MC D-37 enduro in 1978.

PHOTOS: KAREL KRAMER

RIDING HIGH-SPEED FIRE ROADS

BY MARK KARIYA

Riding fire roads can be fun," Honda's Johnny Campbell says. "You get to go really fast, but you have to be careful because of the speed. Sometimes surprises can come up on you—a rain rut, a ditch, a cattle guard, a mud puddle or a blind rise with a blind corner."

In the accompanying photos, we'll show you how the three-time Baja 1000 winner approaches blind rises which often hide blind corners. He also has other tips, like ones dealing with bike setup.

Contrary to popular belief, for example, Campbell doesn't run the rear axle as far back as it'll go in order to gain as much wheelbase as he can on his Honda XR. "On the bigger four-strokes I actually keep the rear wheel as far up as I can in the chain adjusters," he reveals. "That makes it more controlled in sliding and acceleration; the bike is a tighter package and doesn't become so wallowy."

Though Campbell races with stiffer suspension than the average play rider would use, he'd recommend relatively soft suspension settings for the dual-sport fire roader. "Use a little cushier suspension setting—for traction and comfort," he advises. "Lots of fire-roading guys will do a dual-sport ride, and you want to be comfortable; you don't want to be fighting the bike, so you want to have a plush enough setting that you're not getting beat up all day."

He continues, "You want a nice, smooth power delivery—power character—something that's not going to be fighting you all day with a hard-hitting powerband. On the XR650R I don't [drop the fork tubes]; it's pretty standardized, and I usually leave it stock."

1 "When I'm standing and riding a fire road, I usually have my head up over the handlebar. I sit down if it's safe to, where I don't have to look that far out and I can see the road and the terrain. I usually keep one finger on the front brake and my foot hovering over the rear brake. To scrub speed, I use more of the front brake than the rear. I've just developed that technique myself over the years. I do use the rear brake to scrub speed, but I mostly use it to set up for a corner. You apply the rear brake to get the bike into a two-wheeled drift and slide into a corner. So most of the slowing is done with the front and then you use the rear to set up for the corner and get the bike positioned [correctly] in order to get back on the throttle as soon as you can."

2&3 This particular rise comes in a right-hand bend and hides a tighter left-hand corner. "Normally, you stay on the right side of the road," Campbell points out; any oncoming traffic will be on the left-hand side of the rider to avoid head-on collisions. As you can see here, though, Campbell's setting up for this rise by letting himself drift out to the left side of the road.

Why drift to the opposite side of the road? It actually positions him so he can see farther over and around the rise. Notice that he's also standing as he approaches the rise. This helps him see farther ahead—vital as speeds climb. If he did spot oncoming traffic, he could spot it sooner and veer back to the right.

4 As Campbell crests the rise, he is well on his way to swinging to the right side of the road. He'll see that there's no oncoming traffic and will now set up for the left-hand turn that follows. This sweeping arc is a classic road racing line and allows him to maintain more speed than if he hugged the right side of the road the whole way. Following this sort of arc is thus not only relatively safer because it permits Campbell to see farther ahead, but it's faster. How can you beat that?

PHOTOS: MARK KARIYA

Hills

CHAPTER SIX

Ty Davis: Squat to scale slick, steep hills 121
Kevin Hines: Uphill rock jump 122
Dick Burleson: Simple stairstep techniques 123
Hawkins on clutch-control climbs 124
Downhills with Destry Abbott 125
Turning on a hill you can't climb with Ty Davis 126

TY DAVIS:
SQUAT TO SCALE SLICK, STEEP HILLS

One particular hill in the desert near Ty Davis's home is a bear. Since it's dry most of the year, its steep, hard-packed surface is slick; the trail up it is S-shaped. More than sheer horsepower, finesse is required to crest this thing.

Team Green's Davis, the AMA National Enduro Champion, knows finesse. The way he zipped up and down the hill time after time while we shot photos provided graphic evidence of that. Davis also insists that gear selection is critical. "It all depends on the steepness of the hill. If you're [in too low a gear], the revs will be high and you won't be going anywhere. Too high a gear and it will be bogging, so you need to find a happy medium."

We asked Davis to share his secrets (and also critique Joel Smith's failed attempts on Davis's KX500).

RIGHT

1 "I'm looking ahead to try to find the smoothest line possible, since the hill is pretty steep," Davis begins. "I'm in a squat position just in case I accidentally hit a rock, so I can absorb the impact with my knees. My body is in the middle [of the bike] and my head is over the front wheel so it won't wheelie. At the same time, [with] my weight back, I'm getting maximum traction. I have my hand on the clutch just in case it wheelies: I'll pull it in a little to drop the front end, then I'll let it out easy, keeping the throttle three-quarters- to wide-open the whole time."

2 "Since I'm traversing the hill (the trail cuts across the face of it here), I've shifted my weight to weight down the outside footpeg, and keep the rear wheel from sliding or spinning out. My weight is a little further over the front end because the hill is getting steeper, and I don't want to wheelie over backwards."

3 "I'm moving around on the bike to where I get good traction [and still] keep the front end down. Keeping my body over the bike is a key thing," Davis points out. "If I happen to get stuck here, I'm in a good position to jump to the high (uphill) side of the bike and keep it from sliding down the hill on top of me. Never, never, never jump to the downside of the bike! Remember: attack position."

4 "I'm shifting my body to the high side of the hill and maintaining my drive, never shutting off. Remember: Try to stay in the squat position so you can keep the bike moving forward," he concludes.

WRONG

1 "Joel is not looking up the hill to see where he needs to go," Davis notes. "He's not gripping the bike [with his knees]; someone forgot to tell him he's riding a Kawasaki, not a cow-asaki. [He] needs to be over the front end more because the front wheel is starting to lift. [He's] a little to the high side of the hill, which is good."

2 "His weight is too far back. He needed to start traversing the hill instead of rolling off the throttle. If his weight were over [the front of] the bike, he wouldn't have had to let off the gas to keep the front end down. Basically, his fun ticket is now punched."

3 "Weight is [still] too far back. Elbows seem to be down. Needs to be in a squat position. Needs to pick up his foot and put pressure on the pegs so the [rear] tire will get maximum traction."

4 "[Joel's weight] needs to be on the high side of the bike so that when he stalls, he won't let my bike slide to the bottom [of the hill] upside-down. He needs to stop right there and try it again. No attack position. He's lost his balance. Now he's wondering how bad it's going to hurt—not from the crash, from me!"

KEVIN HINES: UPHILL ROCK JUMPS

Fast, rocky uphills are generally no problem: You simply hit them with speed and sail. You can make your trip up the hill a lot smoother if you take to the air. Done correctly you won't lose momentum, and by avoiding the pounding from the rocks, you'll find it reduces fatigue.

What's not to like about this method?

We asked former AMA National Enduro Champion Kevin Hines to demonstrate how it's done when we discovered this particular hill sitting in our way after a turn in the trail.

1 "As soon as I'm in the turn, I'm looking far ahead," Hines begins. "I'm looking up until I can't see [where the trail goes] anymore. I can only see to the top of the hill, so I'm focusing on getting up to the top as fast as possible. I can see rocks, roots, uneven terrain—but I can [also] see a bump at the bottom of the hill. I can carry a lot of speed, come out of the corner and go second to third gear."

2 "What I do is hit the bump—which is about half to three-quarters of the way up the hill—and I preload. I push down on my suspension, hit the bump and lighten up. I am using the clutch, just a [quick slip as I lighten up]. It takes some practice to get that right, but that's something you can practice anywhere, even in your own yard."

3 "If I feel I'm coming up a little short [of the intended landing zone], I'll lift my feet right off the pegs so I can bring the bike up even higher."

4 "I'm landing up over on the top of the hill, missing a lot of rough objects that waste energy and time."

PHOTOS: MARK KARIYA

DICK BURLESON
SIMPLE STAIRSTEP TECHNIQUE

Stairstep sections are aptly named. Made of rock, they pound both bike and rider, and rob precious momentum if you're forced to climb them.

This section of stairsteps on Michigan's Drummond Island is neither steep, nor are the steps themselves spaced too closely, so they provide the novice with a fairly easily surmountable challenge. To demonstrate how an expert would approach the section, we turned to eight-time AMA National Enduro Champion Dick Burleson. After all, who better to ask than a pro?

1 "This stairstep is real rocky and pretty irregular," Burleson begins. "There's a lot of loose rock, and it's at a little bit of an angle to the trail. As I approach it, I stand on the pegs, pretty centered on the bike and in third gear. I look up ahead a lot and try to find a path that's clean at the bottom so I don't get bounced around and can hit the top step pretty squarely so that the bike won't kick one way or the other.

"Not only am I looking for a place that's square [to my direction of travel] to prevent getting kicked sideways, but my plan is to find a big step at the very beginning, hit it pretty hard and get some lift. With enough lift I could jump the last part of the stairstep. (This particular step wasn't big enough to enable me to totally clear [the section].)"

2 "When I hit the first step, I absorb some of the impact with my legs—I'm getting some bend in my knees. I try to stay off the seat and let the bike work. In case it hits another stairstep, I'll still have some space between my butt and the seat. (A couple times when the bike hit, I had to get my weight back a little bit so that the front wheel could go over the last stairstep.) As the back wheel hits, I transfer my weight forward and let the back of the bike work."

3 "The ideal position is to stay centered. If you hit the steps in too low a gear without momentum, the bike's going to bounce all over the place, and you're going to struggle a lot more. I also hold [the bike] pretty tightly between my legs so that it doesn't jump around from side to side."

HAWKINS ON CLUTCH-CONTROL CLIMBS

The only thing tougher than climbing a slippery hill without a run is making an off-camber turn onto a steep slippery climb. The key to completing this frequently encountered off-road maneuver successfully is clutch and throttle control. Randy Hawkins has some advice on how to handle the situation correctly.

1 "This is a typical scenario: The trail goes down a muddy stream bed, then turns sharply up the bank. There is some soft mud in the stream, so I cut the front end hard, load the rear of the bike and pop the clutch enough to get the front end in the air. You must have control of the clutch with one or two fingers, since you have to keep a grip on the bar, too."

4 "I'm underway by this photo. The throttle is steady and I'm slipping the clutch to keep the bike moving as steadily as I can with little or no wheelspin. This slope is almost all rock covered with soft, wet dirt, yet you see no roost coming from the rear tire. I'm moving slow, but I *am* moving and I won't have to pick the bike up or try this again. This technique takes a lot finesse. To avoid wheelspin on a four-stroke or an open class machine you need to have the engine down low in the powerband—right to the point of stalling. A small bike would really have to be revving. In either case, popping the clutch or shuddering it in and out will make you lose control. A nonslip seat cover is great. In situations like these, you can't afford to let your weight slide back on the bike. When you pull off a climb like this properly, you'll be amazed at how slowly you can go on a steep hill and still keep moving."

2 "I plant my left leg firmly so when I pop the clutch, the rear wheel swings around to the right and the front wheel lofts up the bank. I don't have throttle wide open; I'm holding it steady at one quarter, and I may not let the clutch all the way out, either. I want just enough power to drift the rear wheel around and get the front wheel up the bank."

3 "This photo shows the critical moment for body placement. I use the pivot leg to push the bike totally upright. It's crucial the bike be straight up and down as I begin to climb up the steep bank. Otherwise, with no established berm, the rear end will swing out from under me and I'll end up on my butt in the mud. Here I'm still holding the throttle at a steady opening. The key is to allow your brain to concentrate on as few motions as possible. By holding the throttle steady, I only need to use the clutch to control the bike's forward movement. A steady throttle also makes it easier to judge clutch engagement."

PHOTOS: SCOTT HOFFMAN

PRO RIDING SECRETS

DOWNHILLS

BY MARK KARIYA

Downhills in the desert are usually very technical, low-speed affairs that are guaranteed to speed up your heart rate. They're almost always filled with rocks, for one thing, and those rocks come in every variety: loose/rolling, large boulders and jagged/sharp. Thus, you quickly learn that falling on a downhill extracts a high price in pain and suffering as well as broken or abused motorcycle parts.

Defending AMA National Hare & Hound Series Champion Destry Abbott has some terrific advice when it comes to getting down a hill quickly and safely. Try it, and you'll find that it's not necessary to get off your bike to bulldog it.

Of course, if the particular descent you try is beyond your ability, don't be afraid to swallow your pride and walk the bike down. Work up to it with easier downhills until you're confident of the technique required and how it feels.

1 Here's a view from the top. The trail winds its way down this hill, as is usually the case, so there are twists and turns and off-camber along the way. Obviously, it's also filled with loose rock, adding to the degree of difficulty. It's not like a sand dune where you're simply going to power your way down; it calls for a bit of care and more attention to form.

2 "I drag [both] brakes a little bit," Abbott begins. "I wouldn't hold them on [hard] because then your back end's going to be sliding out [on the rocks]." As you can see here, even on a tricky downhill, the Team Green star uses his front as well as his rear brake. Since it's not extremely steep, he doesn't have to keep his weight extremely far back either; instead, he's fairly centered over the middle of the bike. "I try to look ahead," he adds, "when you're going down a hill so you know what kind of speed you can go down. If it's got a turn, then you know you'd better start slowing down and setting up for that turn because you'll waste more time overshooting the turn if you pick up too much speed."

3 "Basically, just try to ride loose [on the bike]. You don't want to ride real tight going down rocks because if you hit something and you're tight, the bike's going to swap. If you're loose, you can use your legs kind of as another shock [absorber] and let the bike do what it's doing. For instance, when I go down hills, I'm really loose, and the bike does a lot of different things—rocking back and forth or whatever."

4 "Usually, if there's a little bit of a trail where someone's ridden and [there's] not as much [loose] rock, I try to stay on that because you get more traction and better braking than you would on [loose] rock," Abbott reveals. "Try to find smooth lines and try to not make a lot of corners going down [loose], rocky [hills]; try to make a lot of straight lines." But try to avoid the cue ball effect and maintain speed with more flowing arcs through turns, he advises. Also keep the bike as straight up and down as possible to keep it the most stable over loose rocks.

TURNING

ON A HILL YOU CAN'T CLIMB
BY MARK KARIYA

Climbing hills is part of nearly any off-road ride or race. Sooner or later, though, everyone will encounter at least one hill that stymies them. Whatever the reason, every dirt rider will eventually need to figure out the best course of action.

Since Yamaha's Ty Davis has a good deal more talent than the average collection of weekend warriors, we pointed him up a nasty knoll to demonstrate how a pro would turn around on such a hill. Besides being extremely steep, this hill is fairly soft and has a slight rut in the trail.

Follow along and remember his advice the next time you find yourself in such a predicament.

1 As on any hill, you want to attack it aggressively but in control. This becomes more important the more technical the hill is. Remain seated, keep your head far forward and hold your elbows up to weight the front end so the bike will be less wheelie-prone. Remember that it's usually better to feather the clutch than shut it off if the front starts coming up.

2 Davis knows he won't make it completely up the hill. Rather than wasting time and energy trying to milk a few more feet out of the attempt, he picks a place to dismount—preferably to the left side. "When you can't make it, you jump off to the side, grab your front brake and turn your front wheel—it helps hold you there until you get situated," he advises.

3 It's probably safest if you kill the engine but leave it in gear; that'll act as a rear brake as long as you don't pull the clutch in. You need to make sure that the bike won't roll backward down the hill unexpectedly the moment you let go of the front brake. The next step is to get turned around.

PHOTOS: MARK KARIYA

4 Davis is a firm believer in keeping the front wheel on the trail as much as possible, so he recommends letting the bike lean into you then picking up the rear with the right hand and right leg. Make sure your left foot is planted firmly into the hill and let the front end turn left to help swing the bike in your direction. "You want to keep your front wheel on the trail so that once you get turned around, you can get back on it and head down," he says.

5 Davis has successfully maneuvered the rear of the bike off the trail. From here, he'll grab the front brake and wiggle the handlebar back and forth to help slide the front wheel down the hill—right where he wants to aim it. If he had let the front of the bike wander off the trail, Davis would have to expend considerably more energy pulling the entire bike back to put the front wheel on the trail.

6 Once pointed downhill, he'll hop aboard and ride back down the hill—undoubtedly to try to climb it again. Keep these final words of advice in mind, though: "If you know you're not going to make it, start planning for exiting in a safe manner! I knew I wasn't going to get up to that last rocky chute, so I just jumped off before I got myself into a bad [situation], turned the bike around and headed down."

126

INDEX

Abbott, Destry, 88, 89, 125
Accelerating out of turns, 22
Airing out off-road, 56
Anatomy of the perfect jump, 54, 55
Avoid getting buried, 11
Avoiding trees in turns, 20
Body position, 96
Brake slide turns, 32
Braking tricks, 59
Braking, 98
Burleson, Dick, 18, 110, 112, 123
Campbell, Johnny, 117, 119
Carmichael, Ricky, 91
Clutch control climbs, 124
Cold Weather riding tips, 71-74
Concrete starts, 13
Cooper, Guy, 30, 63-68, 79, 106
Cornering, 26
Craig, Mike, 51
Crossing logs, 110
Cutting corners, 28, 29
Davis, Ty, 46, 56, 69, 121, 126
Dowd, John, 48
Downhill doubles, 48
Downhill ruts leading into a turn, 25
Downhill starts, 12
Downhills, 125
Drop-offs, 57, 115
Edmondson, 70
Emergency line changes, 33
Emig, Jeff, 45, 47
Ferry, Tim, 91
Flying low, 49
Front-wheel landings, 47
Hatch, Steve, 8, 9, 27, 34, 92
Hawkins, Randy, 19, 90
High-speed turns, 30
Hills, 120-126
Hines, Kevin, 20, 105, 111, 113, 122
Hoffman, Scott, 103
Holeshot tips, 7-9
Hot tips, 58-102
Hot weather riding tips, 75
How to tackle nasty corners, 24
Hughes, Ryan, 40
Inside line, 50

Jumps, 38-57 99
Kicker lips, 44
Kramer, Karl, 103
Lafferty, Mike, 32
Lamson, Steve, 15, 39, 4
Larocco, Mike, 33
Line choice, 79
Maintaining momentum in turns, 15
McGrath, Jeremy, 7, 17, 21, 22, 35, 41, 59
Mid-air turning, 21
Mud ditches, 116
Night advice, 93
Nylander, Bryan, 103
Obstacles, 52
Powder surfing, 62
Prep tips, 60, 61
Railing sand berms, 16
Restarting after a stall, 64
Roeseler, Larry, 69
Rolling jumps, 46
Rutted jumps, 45
Rutted turns, 31
Sand washes, 88
Seat bounce jumps, 51
Speed secrets, 97
Stairstep techniques, 123
Standing-to-seated transitions for turns, 18
Starts, 6-13
Sticking flat corners with jumps, 36
Summers, Scott, 23, 25, 37, 107-109
Suspension, 82-86
Technical cornering technique, 17
Trails, 104-120
Turning techniques, 97
Turns in tight woods, 27
Turns, 14-37
Undercut, banked turns, 23
Uphill jumps, 39
Uphill switchbacks, 114
Vohland, Tallon, 53
Ward, Larry, 16, 52
Wheelying, 65, 68
Whoops, 41, 89
Windham, Kevin, 50, 57, 91
Woods cornering tactics, 19
XR600R, 107, 108

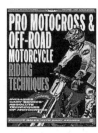

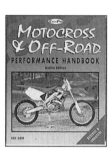
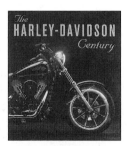
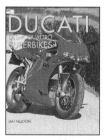